THE TWO SIEGES OF RHODES
1480–1522

THE TWO SIEGES
OF RHODES

1480–1522

Eric Brockman

JOHN MURRAY

XV mile the sea brode is
From Turkey to the Ile of Rodez . . .
And on a hull there alle alonen,
Is a Castell stiff and strong.
The Castell hight men saie soo
Sancta Maria de Fulmaro [Phileremo] . . .
A strong toun Rodez hit is,
The Castell is strong and fair I wis . . .

MATHEW PARIS: *Purchas His Pilgrimes*

Printed in Great Britain for
John Murray, Albemarle Street, London
by Cox & Wyman Ltd, London
Fakenham and Reading
7195 1894 6

CONTENTS

ILLUSTRATIONS

ILLUSTRATIONS

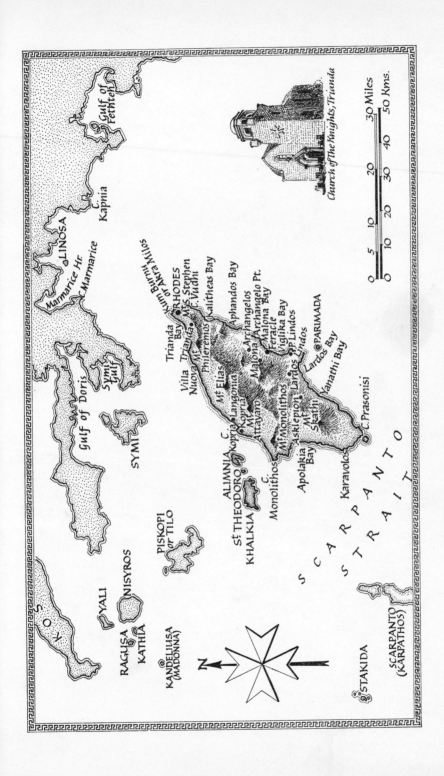

Church of the Knights, Trianda

KOS

YALI

RAGUSA
KATHÁ

NISYROS

KANDELIUSA
(MADONNA)

PISKOPI
or TILO

SYMI

Gulf of Doris

Symi
Gulf

LINOSA

C. Marmarice
Marmarice Hr.

C.
Kapnia

Gulf of
Fethteh

St THEODORO

ALIMNIA
C.

KHALKIA

Monolithos

C.

Kopria
Langonia

Mt
Attavaro

Villa

Nuova Mt.

Mt Elias

Philerémos

Trianda
Bay

Kum Burnu
or Akra Milos

RHODES

Mt. Stephen
C. Vudni

Kallitheas Bay

Aphandos Bay

Archangelos

Malona Archangelo Pt.

Feracle

Malona
Bay

Viglika Bay

Pt Lindos

Mt Monolithos

Asklepion Lardos

Mt
Skathi

Lindos

Lardos

PARIMADA

Vanathi Bay

Apolakia
Bay

Karavolo

C. Prasonisi

SCARPANTO

STRAIT

STAKIDA

SCARPANTO
(KARPATHOS)

N

30 Miles

50 Kms.

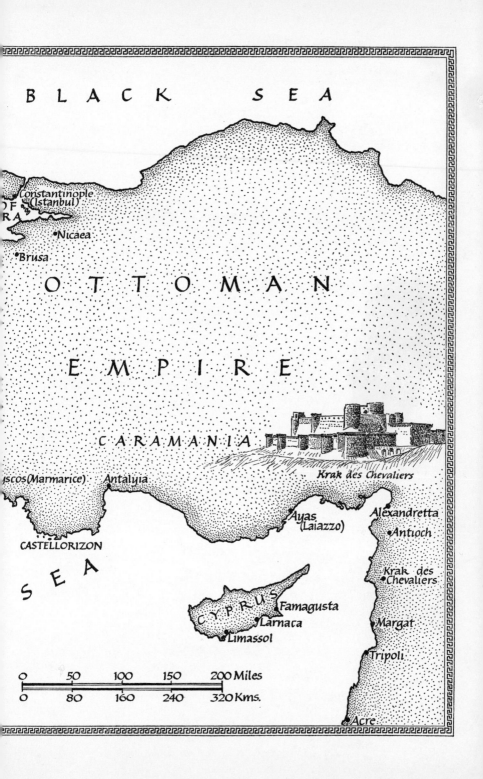

BLACK SEA

Constantinople
(Istanbul)

•Nicaea

•Brusa

OTTOMAN

EMPIRE

CARAMANIA

Krak des Chevaliers

scos(Marmarice) Antalyia

Ayas
(Laiazzo)

Alexandretta

•Antioch

CASTELLORIZON

•Krak des
Chevaliers

SEA

CYPRUS •Famagusta

•Larnaca

•Margat

•Limassol

•Tripoli

0   50   100   150   200 Miles
0   80   160   240   320 Kms.

•Acre

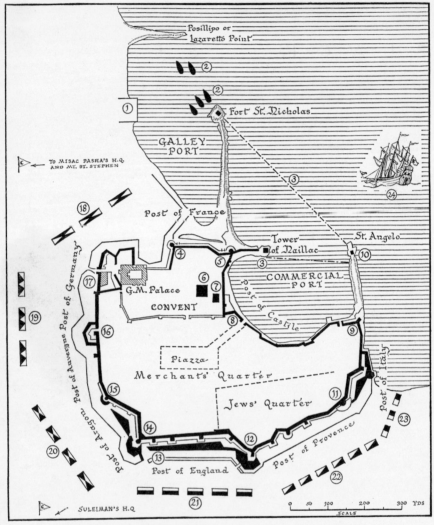

RHODES — 1480/1522

KEY
1. Turkish Batteries – 1480
2. Blockships – 1522
3. Boom Defence – 1522
4. St. Paul's Gate
5. St. Peter's Gate
6. Arsenal
7. 'Inn' of England
8. Sea Gate
9. St. Catherine's Gate
10. Tower of the Windmills
    (or St. Angelo)
11. Tower of Italy
12. St. John's
    (or Koskino) Gate

13. St. Anthony's Gate
14. St. Mary's Tower
15. Tower of Aragon (Spain)
16. Tower of St. George
17. D'Amboise Gate
18. Bali Agha and Janissaries – 1522
19. Ayas Pasha – 1522
20. Ahmed Pasha – 1522
21. Qasim Pasha – 1522
22. Mustafa Pasha – 1522
23. Pir Pasha – 1522
24. Cortoglu – 1522

(Defences relate to 1522)

INTRODUCTION

Gibbon's well-worn comment that the Knights Hospitallers 'neglected to live but were prepared to die in the service of Christ' invites the retort that all too few of their contemporaries were ready to do either.

It might be said of the fall of Rhodes in 1522, as has been said of the fall of Constantinople, that it was a symbolic event rather than an historical landmark. The Ottoman Turks had long been in Europe and nothing short of a new crusade could drive them back. With Rhodes and its island dependencies, there fell into Muslim hands the fortress of St. Peter, near Halicarnassus, the last Christian sovereignty anywhere on the mainland of the eastern Mediterranean. When, centuries later, European navies and armies returned to this part of the world, they did not come essentially as Christians, nor even as Europeans.

The Hospitallers were the last of the crusaders. They were also the last of the Europeans, and they differed from their contemporaries – and from many of us – in three notable respects. They put loyalty to their faith and to their Order before all other loyalties. They welcomed death as a gateway to eternal life, and they sought valiantly to sustain the hope that Europe might yet lead and convert the world.

If we are tempted to condemn their choice of the sword, their arrogance and their pride, and their tendency to 'hate the sinner, not the sin', we should recall that few men ever completely transcend the standards of their times. Words like faith, honour, duty, have different meanings – or none at all – to different generations.

The story of the two sieges of Rhodes – of the resounding victory of the Hospitallers over the Greek-led armada of Mehmet the Conqueror in 1480, and their defeat at the hands of young Suleiman the Magnificent in 1522, from which little was salved but honour – has been told repeatedly over the four centuries and more which have passed since then. But it is, I believe, a story which deserves re-telling, not only for itself, but because it is

I

a part of the larger story to which Constantinople (1453), Malta (1565), Lepanto (1571) and Vienna (1683) belong.

There are first-hand accounts of both sieges. William Caoursin, who was in Rhodes throughout the siege of 1480 and was Vice-Chancellor of the Order of St. John, published his Latin record in Venice towards the end of 1480. He also compiled an official record of the Order's part in the remarkable tragedy of the young Ottoman pretender Djem. An English translation of Caoursin's Latin by John Kaye, laureate of King Edward IV, was published by Caxton in 1496.

Another eye-witness of 1480 was the bellicose Augustinian Fra. Giacomo de Curti, who wrote an Italian account in a letter to his brother in Venice, also published in 1480. His lively day-to-day commentary is somewhat marred by repeated interruptions in his narrative when, according to him, the people sang a number of excellent psalms of his own composition, which he quotes at length.

Then there is the Grand Master Pierre D'Aubusson's own report, written from Rhodes to the Emperor Frederick III very soon after the departure of the defeated Palaeologos Pasha.

The Italian historiographer Enrico Pantaleone included detailed accounts of both sieges in a history of the Hospitallers published at Basle in 1581. He cannot have been present at either siege; but his gossipy style suggests first-hand sources other than Caoursin or de Curti.

For 1522, there is the personal story of the Chevalier Jacques de Bourbon, published in French at Paris in 1526, and that of Jacobus Fontanus (Jacob Fonteyn), the Flemish jurist and Judge of the Appeal Court of Rhodes. Fontanus's account, dedicated to the Hospitaller Pope Clement VII, was published in Rome in 1524.

There is also the Cotton MS. letter of Sir Nicholas Roberts, written from Messina in May 1523 to his kinsman the Earl of Surrey: a model of English understatement.

The standard authorities are Bosio (1594) and Vertot (1796). English writers of the nineteenth and early twentieth centuries like Taafe, Porter, Sutherland and King, rely mainly on these two sources for their versions of the sieges. King is notable for having disentangled English names and references from their latinized disguises, and thus added greatly to our appreciation of the English part in the fighting.

Of several Turkish accounts, none, it seems, is by an eye-witness. The best are Sa'ad ud-Din for 1480, and Mustafa Gelal-Zade for 1522. Ettore Rossi's translations from the Turkish into Italian, upon which I have relied, are most useful for tidying up the tangled chronology of the European accounts.

In such details as dates and times of day, weather and weapons, where the original accounts disagree (as they invariably do), I have chosen the most probable; but I have not included any incident or conversation for which there is not at least some authority.

I have tried to set the two principal scenes against their background in time. This has led to a somewhat lengthy 'prologue'; but it seems to me that without some such setting of the stage, any relatively brief part of the thousand-year-old history of the Knights Hospitallers of St. John is apt to appear as in a vacuum, and only makes sense for the specialist or the professional.

In the spelling of personal names I have generally preferred the least confusing version; but where other spellings help to distinguish a character I have not tried to be consistent. For place names I have adhered to the nomenclature of the Admiralty charts, unless an alternative is better known.

Acknowledgements are due to the Trustees of the British Museum for permission to reproduce the portrait of Suleiman II; to the National Gallery for the portrait of the Sultan Mehmet; to Sir Hannibal Scicluna for continual reference to his library; to Major Edward Scicluna, whose unerring nose for a picture helped to track down the little known portrait of Tadini da Martinengo; to Captain Charles Zammit, F.S.A., Director of the Malta National Museum, for the line drawings and for much other help; to Mr. George Fabri, Chairman of the Malta Government Tourist Board, for photographs of frescoes in the Palace in Valletta; to Madame Tsimbouki of Rhodes for a number of valuable suggestions; to Mr. John R. Murray and Mr. Jeremy Steele for much editorial help; and last, but not least, to Professor Lionel Butler of St. Andrews

University for his painstaking advice. My personal thanks are also due to Mrs. Theresa Briffa, who deciphered my handwriting.

ERIC BROCKMAN

San Martin
Malta

PROLOGUE

We are now free to turn our arms against the Turks. . . . We . . .
will lay down our life for our flock since in no other way can
we save the Christian religion from being trampled by the
forces of the Turk. We will equip a Fleet as large as the resources of the Church will permit. We will embark, old as we
are, and racked with sickness. We will set our sails and voyage
to Greece and Asia . . .[1]

These are the words of Pope Pius II – Aeneas Silvius Picco-
lomini – uttered shortly before he set out for Ancona on the last
of his many travels in the year 1464. He was dying. As his litter
approached the port his attendants drew the curtains so that he
should not see the hundreds of deserters from his fleet hurrying
homewards.

He had been full of hope. At Mantua, four years earlier, he had
reviewed the Christian scene:

If the Hungarians receive aid they will attack the Turks
energetically with all their forces. The Germans promise an
army of 42,000 fighting men, Burgundy 6,000. The Italian
clergy with the exception of the Venetians and the Genoese will
contribute a tenth and the laity a thirtieth of their income; the
Jews a twentieth of their possessions . . . the Ragusans will
furnish two galleys, the Rhodians four. . . . The Venetians,
although they have promised nothing publicly, when they see
the Crusade actually ready will surely not fail us nor endure to
seem inferior to their ancestors. We can say the same of the
French, the Castilians and the Portuguese. England, now racked
with civil war, holds out no hope, nor does Scotland, remote
as it is at Ocean's farthest bounds. Denmark, Sweden and
Norway also are too far away to be able to send soldiers and
they have no money to contribute, as they are content with fish
alone. The Poles, who border the Turks along Moldavia, will
not dare to desert their own cause. The Bohemians we shall be
able to hire; they will not fight outside their own country at

their own expense. Such is the situation of the Christian cause. Italian money will equip a fleet, if not at Venice, then in Genoa or in Aragon, and it will not be smaller than the occasion requires. The Hungarians will arm 20,000 cavalry and as many infantry. These, with the Germans and the Burgundians, will make 88,000 soldiers in the field. Does anyone think that the Turks will not be conquered with these forces? They will be joined by George Skanderbeg and a very strong force of Albanians, and many all over Greece will desert from the enemy. In Asia Charamanus and the Armenians will attack the Turks in the rear. We have no reason to despair if only God Himself will favour our undertaking.[2]

Pius's estimate of 88,000 troops from Hungary, Burgundy and Germany was greatly inflated, either from the usual hyperbole of the times or from wishful thinking.

But all these bold hopes came to less than nothing. Only Venice and the Knights Hospitallers of Rhodes went to war. Venice lost Dalmatia, Lemnos and Morea to the Turks. The spirit of the true crusade, the motives which had inspired Saint Louis and Richard Lionheart, had long been blurred. Pius himself, a typical son of the Renaissance, saw more clearly than most that western civilization was threatened with annihilation; but even if his final act was inspired by religious dedication, his thinking had never been devoid of practical, economic elements.

By the fifteenth century few Christians any longer saw a crusade as a simple matter of recovering the Holy Places from Islam, or of expelling the Crescent from the confines of the old Roman Empire, of carrying the Cross into Asia, or even of suppressing heresy. Christendom, so far as the name any longer had meaning, was beset by the new and less benign fever of nationalism, and for the next three centuries the Christian nations of the west were to fight on the eastern frontiers only when they were frightened. And their motives were more often commercial than religious. Nevertheless, the old religious fervour still burned in a few hearts, and the story of Rhodes is about men of the minority which was to save western civilization in spite of itself.

If the crusades were ended, the counter-crusade, which Muslim writers[3] see as their natural outcome, was still in flood. Since the birth of Islam in the seventh century, in a remote part of Arabia, the followers of that faith had irrupted into every part of the known world. First the Arabs had been converted, then Syrians, Egyptians and Moors, Berbers and Negroes, Persians and Indians – even distant Mongols and Tartars and Indonesians – and they had spread Islam and its power into lands and amongst peoples of whom Mahomet had never heard. They believed their conquests to be necessary as part of the Jihad – the Holy War which was to bring salvation to all men. This much they had in common with the crusaders.

Yet orthodox Islam did not always approve of the violent Jihad. Arab philosophers recognized three kinds of 'jihad', or 'striving'. These were the individual, personal striving for perfection; the striving for converts by spreading the Word of God, and by example and argument; and – least commendable – the striving by the sword. War against unbelievers in general, and against Latin Christians in particular, was justified on the familiar grounds of the defence of their faith and fear of 'encirclement'.

Mehmet the Conqueror was anxious at least to appear magnanimous. At the siege of Constantinople in 1453 he offered terms 'partly to show that he was not unreasonable, and partly to satisfy his own conscience as a good Muslim who should avoid fighting unless the Infidel obstinately refused to surrender'.[4]

Suleiman the Magnificent ('the Lawgiver', as the Turks call him) justified his attack on Rhodes not only because of the 'hurt and loss of Islam sustained at the hands of the worst of Infidels', but also 'because it was his duty, as Caliph, to guide humanity and to attempt to cure its many imperfections'.[5]

When Pope Pius II died in 1464 Islam controlled the greater part of the territories of the former Byzantine Empire and all the states (which the Franks called 'Outremer') founded by the crusaders: Egypt, Syria, Persia, and the whole of the north African littoral; the Moorish kingdom of Granada in Spain, as well as great tracts of distant Asia and India. There had been setbacks. The Normans had recovered Sicily and southern Italy in the eleventh century and the Franks and the Spaniards had pushed the Crescent almost out of western Europe. There were also pockets of Christian resistance in the eastern Mediterranean. Venice held several important areas in Greece besides the islands of Negropont (Euboea), Crete and Corfu; while the Ionian Islands were nominally independent, and the Knights Hospitallers of St. John held Rhodes, Kos and some other strongholds in the Dodecanese and on the coast of Asia Minor. The Genoese settlements at Chios and in the Black Sea were tolerated by the Turks, and Cyprus was also nominally independent, though in practice tributary to Egypt.

But Islam was not united, and the Muslim advance had been almost as bedevilled by schism and tribal and dynastic feuds as had Christendom. If, to a western Christian, the schismatics of the Byzantine Empire were 'less pardonable and more to be condemned than the false worship of the conquering Ottoman',[6] the same might be said of the Sunnite Muslim in the eyes of a Shi'ite; and to the culture of Arabic Islam – a synthesis of the intellectual achievements of the ancient world – the Turks were Asiatic barbarians and never very good Muslim.

Nevertheless, it was for the Turks – an Asiatic nomadic race, divided by their wanderings into a host of tribes and generally supposed to be the same people as the Huing-Nu, who for so long troubled the Chinese Empire and compelled the building of the Great Wall – to found and to sustain the one great and lasting empire in the history of Islam.

Our story is concerned with a particular Turkish tribe, the 'Othman' or Ottoman Turks. Othman, the founder of a line which was to threaten the world with its power, was by some accounts a simple Bithynian herdsman who became an Emir under the Seljuk Sultan and, after 1307, himself an independent prince. Gradually encroaching on Byzantine territory, Othman resorted to open war in 1299, occupying several strategic points between Brusa and Nicaea. In 1301 he beat the Byzantines at Nicomedia, and in 1326 occupied Brusa. The organization of the Ottoman Turkish state is due to Othman's son Orkhan, who married Theodora, a daughter of the Greek Emperor John VI, and set up his capital at Brusa, where he proceeded to create a nation and perfect a military organization in comparison with which most European armies were still a disorganized rabble. He fought the Byzantines and the Seljuks simultaneously, capturing

8

Nicaea and Nicomedia from the Greeks, and Pergamus and the province of Mysia from the Seljuks.

Suleiman I, Orkhan's successor, crossed the Hellespont into Europe and was buried in Gallipoli. He was the first Ottoman prince to be buried in European soil, and his tomb 'invited the races of Asia to perform their pilgrimage to it with the sword of conquest'.[7] He was succeeded by Murad I who pushed into the Balkans, capturing Adrianople and Demotika in 1361, and threatening Constantinople. Christendom was alarmed into talk of a crusade; but nothing came of it, and the Greek Emperor was compelled to recognize the Ottoman conquests. Murad pressed on into Europe, taking Monastir in 1380, Sofia in 1385, and falling at last in the hour of victory at Kossovo, stabbed in his tent by a Serbian patriot in 1389.

The Ottoman impetus was not halted by Murad's death. His successor, Bajazet I, called 'Yilderim' (the Thunderbolt) occupied Thessaly in 1391 and annihilated a crusading army at Nicopolis in 1396. But Bajazet was not to pursue his great aim of conquering Constantinople. His name 'was for many centuries the standing example of the mutability of human fortune'.[8] His army was overrun by a new wave of Asiatic conquerors under Timur Lenk (Timur the Lame) at Angora in 1402. Timur Lenk was himself a Turk, but descended from Jengis Khan on his mother's side. He had made himself master of Delhi, Samarcand, Baghdad and Damascus; but his momentum was spent, and his conquests had reached their limit.

Bajazet was captured and, by some accounts, exposed in an iron cage until he died, leaving his sons to fight for the remains of his empire. This was the moment when Christendom might have united and driven the Turks out of Europe and beyond the confines of the ancient Roman Empire; but Christendom was in turmoil. The Church was virtually powerless and terribly wounded by the schism of the Papacy until 1417. The chivalry of England and France were still locked in their seemingly endless struggle. Italy was torn apart by the feuding of Venice and Milan and a host of petty despots. The Turks were given a long breathing-space and were fortunate in that space to have two sultans of the calibre of Mehmet I and Murad II.

Not until the rise of the Hungarian John Hunyadi was any

serious attempt made to deal with the Turkish menace. Then, in 1444, a great alliance of Hungary, Poland, Serbia, Wallachia, Burgundy, Genoa, Venice, the Greek Emperor and the Pope, led by Hunyadi, inflicted a series of crushing defeats on the Turks and compelled them to sue for peace. This was the second opportunity in a generation to destroy the Ottomans. The Christians were within sight of the Turkish capital at Adrianople. A Frankish fleet was in the Hellespont. Skanderbeg and his Albanians and the Seljuk Emirs of Anatolia were in revolt. But Hunyadi – perhaps bribed – made a truce. Then, in November 1444, having broken the truce, he was defeated at Varna. Four years later, his Wallachian allies deserting to the enemy, he was routed at the fated valley of Kossovo.

Little now stood between the Ottomans and the conquest of Constantinople. Western aid for the encircled Byzantine Emperor Constantine XI would only come at the price of 'Henotikon' – submission to the Latin Church – and many of his subjects wondered whether absorption into the Turkish Empire might not be preferable to their present state of division, poverty and impotence. As to 'Henotikon', one of Constantine's most able statesmen, Lucas Notaras, was certain that 'the rule of the Turkish turban was better than that of the Latin mitre'.[9]

Aid, when it came, was too little, and a fortnight too late; and while the Venetians and the Genoese in Constantinople fought bravely when they had no other choice, their home governments were mainly concerned with negotiating favourable commercial arrangements with the Sultan. The Emperor Constantine died a martyr's death on the ramparts, and the Sultan Mehmet behaved with more compassion to the vanquished than many Christians were then displaying to each other.

While the Ottomans went from strength to strength, the Muslim tide was slackening, and even receding, to the south and the west.

The Mamelukes of Egypt, sitting astride the rich and important route of the spice trade – already threatened by the Portuguese in the Red Sea and Indian Ocean – were no longer of the stuff of Saleh-ed-Din (Saladin), and of the men who had driven the Christians out of Syria and Palestine at Acre in 1291; whose counter-crusade had carried Egyptian rule into Cilician Armenia, and whose power extended from the Nile to the Tigris. Egyptian motives were now more commercial; and it was to protect their trade and to safeguard their supplies of shipbuilding timber, which came principally from the Black Sea ports, that they engaged in war with the Lusignans of Cyprus (who, with the Knights of Rhodes had sacked Alexandria in the 'crusade' of 1365) and with their Genoese and Venetian allies. In 1426 King Janus II of Cyprus was displayed to the people of Cairo in chains. He was ransomed by the Venetians; but Cyprus remained an Egyptian tributary until the marriage of Caterina Cornaro to James III in 1489, when it became a Venetian protectorate and a most lucrative entrepôt for Venetian commerce. As they said of themselves: 'We are Venetians first and Christians second.'

It was no inadvertance on the part of Pius II which omitted all reference to the Egyptians from his crusading speeches. He might safely say that 'Charamanus [the Emir of Caramania] and the Armenians will attack the Turks in the rear'; but he knew that the Egyptian situation was more delicate. The Mamelukes had been as little pleased at Ottoman expansion as the Latins; and their fires were burning low. An attack on the Knights of Rhodes in September 1440 had failed dismally – twelve out of an investing Egyptian fleet of seventeen vessels falling into the hands of the Hospitallers at Castellorizon (Chateauroux). In 1443 the Mamelukes were more successful against Castellorizon; but they again failed in the following year against Rhodes itself, and retired discomfited to negotiate a treaty with the Hospitallers on terms greatly to the Christian advantage.

In the west the Muslim tide had been halted, and was to be turned back by the rise of a new power which was to be called Spain; but at Pius II's death no one might have supposed that any very effective crusade could be expected of the Aragonese, Catalans or Castilians. For ten years Catalonia was to be at war with Aragon. It was to be some thirty years before the Moorish kingdom of Granada fell to the Spanish infantry, and another twenty before Spanish arms had advanced along the north African littoral as far as Algiers.

The fall of Constantinople had been inevitable – failing a full-scale crusade by the Latins. 'An empire consisting of one decaying city could not hold out against an empire whose territory covered the greater part of the Balkan peninsula and of Asia Minor, an empire vigorously governed and provided with the best military machine of the age.'[10] Nevertheless, as the Ottomans understood well, a grand Christian alliance operating from some suitable advanced base might unseat them.[11]

Such a base remained – an anachronism like Byzantium and a freak survival from the First Crusade. The island of Rhodes and its little empire of island fortresses pointed like a spearhead at the heart of Islam: manned by men whose religious zeal was as fierce as that of any Janissary; whose organization, discipline and unity in counsel and action were unique; and who subsisted primarily not on commerce but on such international rents and subventions as the Catholic conscience of Europe permitted them to receive.

By 1480, western Europe was dominated by the two great powers of Spain and of France, where, with the possible exception of England, the ideas of nationhood and nationality had first taken hold. These great Christian peoples ought to have combined against Islam. Instead, they embarked on a series of violent quarrels into which they drew every lesser power, using the Papacy and the spiritual power of the Church as pawns in their ambitious adventures, and Italy as their cockpit.

The marriage of Ferdinand of Aragon and Isabella of Castile in 1469, followed by the absorption of Catalonia, had made Spain a great power. The 'Little Reformation' of Cardinal Ximenes de Cisneros[12] and the warrior Dominicans ensured the survival of a militant, state Catholicism which was peculiarly Spanish. The Muslim had been within Spanish gates for seven centuries, and though now harmless enough, they were still there in the kingdom of Granada. Little wonder that a distant crusade, or the plight of a preponderantly French handful of Knights, should fail to excite much sympathy in the new Spain.

The emergence of France as a rival to a united Spain was ensured by the French Crown's acquisition (in 1477) of Burgundy, Picardy and Artois, and (in 1480) of Maine, Anjou, Provence and Brittany. But, preoccupied with the growing threat of Spanish hegemony and the inherited Aragonese claims in Italy, and still

12

fearful of English claims on French territory, France made no national effort to help Rhodes; but she did number amongst the Hospitallers many of the flower of her knighthood.

Portugal, small and militarily weak in Europe, was busy holding her own in the Iberian peninsula, and was well embarked upon the wonderful tale of maritime adventures which were to found her empire in the East.

England under the Yorkist Edward IV was slowly recovering her potential after the havoc of the Hundred Years War and the civil Wars of the Roses. The more adventurous of her chivalry hurried to the aid of Rhodes; but they were few.

Germany – the Germany of the Empire – was a patchwork of principalities owing a tenuous allegiance to a King Emperor;[13] but a patchwork within which there was a rising consciousness of German nationality. Machiavelli said of the power of Germany that 'none could doubt it . . . for it abounds in men, riches and arms . . . but it is such as cannot be used'.

Eastern Europe from Lithuania to Hungary enjoyed a brief unity under the Polish–Lithuanian family, the Jagiellos; but Lithuania and Poland were in constant danger from the Great Prince of Moscow – Ivan the Great (1462–1505), the founder of Russia. Hungary and Bohemia were seething with dynastic troubles, and Hungary was threatened from both east and west. Eastern Europe's crop of religious reformers had also added to the disunity amongst people whose loyalties were already divided between Latin and Greek obediences and Islam.

The Black Sea was an Ottoman lake. Serbia had disappeared. The Bosnians had embraced Islam. Dalmatia and the Greek archipelago were still disputed between Venice and the Turk – Venice still holding her important bases at Coron and Modon and being content enough with freedom to trade.

As for the Papacy, thirty years after the return to Rome from Avignon, instead of concentrating on reform at home and crusade abroad, they became hypnotized by the Renaissance. It is possible to be too hard on them. They had little money; but they maintained as large a fleet as they could afford, kept up a constant propaganda and were vigorous in any negotiation or mediation with the Turks; and, perhaps, it was not 'shameless and worldly' of Sixtus IV, Pope in 1480, to patronize such great Christian painters as Botticelli and Ghirlandaio. But faith was secondary.

The Grand Master of Rhodes had his agents everywhere amongst the ruins of Christendom. The dispatches which reached him often told of brave intentions, but the message was clear: no great Christian prince would risk a crusade which would lay his homeland open to the rapacity of his neighbours, and his throne to the claims of usurpers.

THE HOLY RELIGION

The origins of the Knights Hospitallers of St. John are shrouded in pious myth, and it is not possible to assign an exact date to the beginning of this Order, whose main, Catholic body survives under the resounding title of the Sovereign Military and Hospitaller Order of St. John of Jerusalem, of Rhodes and of Malta. There were, and are, other Hospitaller Orders of chivalry, devoted to the care of the sick; but the title Hospitaller is now generally understood to refer to the Order of St. John in its several Catholic and post-Reformation forms.

In A.D. 600, one Abbot Probus was bidden by Pope Gregory the Great to set up a hospital in Jerusalem for the care of poor and sick pilgrims, and, in A.D. 800, Charlemagne was encouraged by the Caliph Haroun-al-Raschid (of the *Arabian Nights*) to enlarge and endow it. This hospital survived until A.D. 1000, when the mad Caliph El Hakim razed all the Christian buildings in Jerusalem to the ground, including the Church of the Holy Sepulchre and Charlemagne's hospital. But, at some date before the First Crusade, a body of Amalfitan merchants bought the original site, rebuilt the hospital, and staffed it with Benedictine monks.

When Godfrey de Bouillon, Duke of Lorraine, and his victorious crusaders burst into Jerusalem in 1099, they found the Blessed Gerard, Rector of the Hospital, and his monks caring for the sick and wounded and the poor of all creeds. With Godfrey's help, Gerard broke away from the Benedictine Rule and founded a separate Order, with a Rule based on that of the Augustinians. Gifts and grants of property and lands followed. The earliest grant on record was that of the Seignory of Montboue in Brabant, which came from Godfrey. A Bull of Pope Paschal II, dated at Benevento in 1113, confirmed all the 'Hospitals and Poor Houses of the Order as its sole property in perpetuity . . . either on this side of the water, to wit in Asia, or in Europe, as also those which hereafter by God's bounty it may obtain'; and went on to decree that no property of the Order might be 'rashly disturbed, carried off or retained . . . its revenues diminished . . . harassed or annoyed', threatening the excommunication of any person whether ecclesiastical or secular who should attempt to oppose the provisions of the Bull.

Gerard also acquired the former Greek monastery of St. John the Baptist, and the monks then began to call themselves the Hospitallers of St. John of Jerusalem.

A Provençal called Raymond du Puy succeeded the Blessed Gerard as Master of the Hospital in 1125 (the title Grand Master was first used by Roger des Moulins, an Anglo-Norman, in 1177). Raymond was the author of the Order's first independent Rule, and the originator of its military function, which he adopted in emulation of the Knights of the Temple, or Templars, a purely military Order founded in 1119; but although the Hospitallers of St. John now began to bear arms in defence of the pilgrim routes and the Holy Places, they never ceased to maintain their hospital, or to forget their duty to the sick and the poor of Christ.

Raymond's original Rule, approved by Pope Anastasius IV in 1154, was lost in the Holy Land; but a repetition of its essentials was approved by Pope Boniface VIII in 1300. It reads in part:

> . . . I, Raymond, the Servant of Christ's poor, and Master of the Hospital of Jerusalem . . . have established the following precepts in the House of the Hospital of Jerusalem . . . I desire that all those Brethren who have dedicated themselves to the service of the Poor . . . shall maintain inviolate the three Promises . . . Chastity, Obedience and to live without any property of their own . . .

Throughout the history of the Latin kingdom of Jerusalem the Hospitallers fought in every action against Islam in the Holy Land and its approaches, together with the Templars and, for a time, the Teutonic Knights, who, originally an Hospitaller Order of the Hospital of St. Mary of the Germans in Jerusalem, soon became solely military.

While the three banners of these brotherhoods of fighting monks – the white cross of St. John on its red field, the red cross on white of the Templars and the black cross on white of the Germans – went into battle together, relations between the

Orders were anything but brotherly. The Hospitallers and the Templars, particularly, were at constant loggerheads about knightly precedence and other such worldly affairs. But they all knew how to die.

In 1187, Saladin, having united Egypt and Syria, proclaimed a Jihad and besieged Tiberias in Galilee. A Christian relieving force was destroyed at Kurn Hattin, and more than two hundred Hospitallers and Templars who refused to apostatize to Islam were massacred. Others died when Acre, and then Jerusalem itself, fell to Saladin. Yet the Knights held out in isolated castles like Margat and Krak des Chevaliers. Saladin allowed the Hospitallers twelve months in which to transfer their Convent from Jerusalem to Margat.

For a century fighting went on with intermittent truces, but always with the tide of the Jihad running in favour of Islam, and the Christians failing from lack of unity. In 1191 Acre was recaptured by the Third Crusade led by Richard Cœur de Lion, and the Hospitallers established themselves there, giving the city their name – St. Jean d'Acre. There followed the inglorious episode of the Fourth Crusade, in which the Hospitallers played a small part helping the Venetians to sack Christian Constantinople.

One by one the strongholds of the crusading Orders in the Holy Land fell before the repeated blows of the counter-crusade: Ascalon, Caesarea and Antioch; the Templar castles of Safed and Belfort; the Hospitaller strongholds of Margat and Krak des Chevaliers and, in 1291, the last foothold at St. Jean d'Acre. William de Henley, the Prior of England, with all his English Knights, perished in the burning ruins.

Only seven Knights of St. John escaped alive from Acre,[1] and the remnants of the Hospitallers and their historic rivals, the Templars, retreated to Cyprus.

With the loss of the last Frankish foothold on the mainland of Asia, the whole aim and purpose of these military monks and friars seemed to have disappeared. However, the Teutonic Knights had already found a new *métier* on the north-eastern borders of Europe, where they survived for 230 years as the valued and powerful allies of Poland, and later of the Prussians in their wars against the Baltic pagans and the nascent Orthodox Russians.

In 1225, they had moved their main body into Poland and fought the Prussians. By 1283, they were masters of all the land between Memel and the Vistula. They inherited Livonia and Courland from the extinct Knights of the Sword. After subduing the Prussians they established their Convent in Marienburg and seized Pomerania. Their Bailiwick of Utrecht survives as an association of Protestant noblemen in the Netherlands. Their end, as a Catholic Order of chivalry, came with the election of the Margrave Albrecht of Hohenzollern-Anspach as Grand Master in 1510, whereafter they were amongst the founders of the Prussian state which was to prove so troublesome to Europe.

The Templars – who had been the financiers (and moneylenders) of the Frankish colonies of 'Outremer' and the Holy Land, and had amassed considerable riches all over Europe, but principally in France – were brought to a dismal and probably quite unjust end by the greedy machinations of the French King Philip and his creature the Avignon Pope Clement V at the Council of Vienne in 1312. Their properties eventually passed to the Hospitallers, who gained little immediate benefit from them since they were burdened with all the charges of the protracted legal proceedings against the Grand Master de Molay and the majority of the Templars, as well as with the maintenance of the imprisoned Knights, most of whom were convicted on the flimsiest of evidence of unspeakable blasphemies, heresies, perversions and black magic, and put horribly to death.

In Cyprus, where the Lusignans had inherited the very strict feudal service of the Latin kingdom of Jerusalem – requiring military service of unlimited duration, as opposed to the more common forty days elsewhere – the Hospitallers found themselves tied to the policies of the Lusignans, and the Grand Master William de Villaret, who had succeeded the saintly but ineffectual Odo de Pins, began to mature his plans for the conversion of the Order into a maritime power, virtually independent of any overlord. William died before his plan could be implemented; but Rhodes and its Dodecanese dependencies had already been selected as the target, and Fulk, William's brother, the new Master, hastened to its execution.

Rhodes in 1306 was under the control of a Byzantine governor who had cast off all but a semblance of allegiance to Constantinople and had set up a pirate state which might justifiably be attacked without the leave of the Eastern Emperor. A Genoese adventurer, one Vignolo dei Vignoli, was already 'renting' Kos and Lemnos from the Emperor Andronicus II, and the Hospitallers made a contract with him for a combined assault on Rhodes and such other of the Sporades as they could occupy.

Rhodes was to be handed over to the Order, with the exception of two villages which were to go to Vignolo. Lemnos and Kos were to be ceded to the Order by Vignolo, and he was to be 'Vicar' of all the other islands. Revenues (and the proceeds of Vignolo's piracy) were to be divided: one-third for him and two-thirds for the Order.

The original landing parties disembarked in July 1307. By the end of September only Feracle (Pheraclos or Pheraclyea) had fallen. Mount Phileremos (the ancient Ialysos) was surprised early in November, when a Greek traitor opened an unguarded postern. Legend had it that a body of Knights gained entry with the flocks being driven in at sunset, disguised in sheepskins – a touch sufficiently Homeric that we are at liberty to doubt it. The legend may have arisen from some monkish misreading of a reference to the Knights entering the 'Mandraccio', as the Galley Port was called, since it was also the Greek word for 'sheepfold'. Our Lady of Phileremos (variously spelt Philerimos, Philermo, Filermo) became an important cult with the Order, whose prayer today contains the invocation: 'I most humbly entreat Thee through the intercession of the Most Holy Virgin of Phileremos . . .'

On 5th September 1307, Pope Clement V confirmed the Hospitallers in their possession of Rhodes; but it was to be another two years before they were to secure control of the island; by which time the Order had mortgaged its revenues for twenty years with the Florentine moneylender Peruzzi. The Order's and Vignolo's fleets invested the city of Rhodes; but the Rhodians and their Muslim allies proved tough. At last, Greek reinforcements who had been blown off course and arrived in Cyprus were persuaded by a Cypriot Knight, one Philip le Jaune, to change sides and to press the Rhodians to surrender the city. On 15th August 1309, Rhodes surrendered to the Grand Master Fulk de Villaret.

The Order was now possessed of a satisfactory little feudal state with its own prince, its own tenants in chief, its own *servicia debita* and its own vassals, under no obligation to serve anyone but the Holy Father – and the poor of Christ.

With Rhodes, the Order obtained the suzerainty of Khalkia, Piskopi (or Tilos), Nisyros, Kos (or Lango), Kalymnos, Leros and Symi; and was later to acquire Budrum (or St. Peter) near the site of Halicarnassos on the mainland opposite Kos, and Castellorizon, eighty miles due east of Lindos. And here the Knights were to remain for more than two centuries, astride one of the principal sea routes of the eastern Mediterranean, within striking distance of the valuable timber trade southward from the Black Sea, and the vital spice routes northward and westward from Arabia, not to mention the lucrative local trades in honey, dried fish, grain, wine and silk.

With their fortresses on the eastern extremity of Kos and St. Peter on the mainland opposite, they commanded the whole of the Gulf of Kos and the Kos Channel. Nisyros, Piskopi and Khalkia stood guard over the Gulfs of Doris and Symi. Rhodes city with Lindos, and Castellorizon, very close to the mainland of Caramania, covered the approaches to and from Syria and Egypt. They had, as yet, little to fear from the unseamanlike Egyptians and Ottomans; and they had time and relative security in which to consolidate their new independence, to streamline their administration, to modify Rhodian law to meet the needs of an aristocratic, religious republic, to fortify their possessions and to ensure their sea power. On the whole they used their time well, and the strictures of the Avignon Papacy and others were not justified.

Nevertheless, at various moments throughout the fourteenth and early fifteenth centuries, the Hospitallers were in some danger of being suppressed as the Templars had been. The properties which they had acquired throughout Europe excited the cupidity of princes and pontiffs, always short of ready cash for their own dubious adventures; while the Venetians, in particular, were apt to regard the Order as a nuisance and a rival only a little less serious than Genoa.

Writers like Marino Sanudo in the fourteenth century and Emmanuele Piloti in the fifteenth criticized the Hospitallers for not making proper use of their resources. Sanudo, a Venetian, attacked the Order in a letter to the Pope dated February 1329, and accused them of harbouring pirates in Rhodes. Piloti was a Cretan of Venetian origin who had travelled widely in the Middle East and held strong views about a new crusade. In 1420 he published his treatise 'De modu progressu ordine ac diligenti providentia habendis in passagio Christianorum pro conquesta terre sancte'.[2] King Jaime II of Aragon predicted, in 1309, that the Hospitallers 'would establish themselves in Rhodes solely to serve their own interests'.[3]

The Papal Curia at Avignon was particularly vehement in its denunciations. In August 1343 Clement VI wrote to the Grand Master threatening 'reforms' and the foundation of a new crusading order, and rebuking him for the misapplied wealth of the Hospital, the luxury, houses, hounds, falcons, dress, food and gold and silver appurtenances of Rhodes. Innocent VI uttered similar threats in 1355. The poet Petrarch wrote in 1352 of 'Rhodes, shield of the Faith, lying unwounded, inglorious'.[4]

But the wealth was exaggerated. It had taken the Order years to pay off the immense debts incurred in the subjugation of Rhodes and its dependencies.[5] The Florentine banks, in which much of the Order's treasure was invested, collapsed in 1340, and throughout the latter half of the fourteenth century rents fell everywhere in Europe.

In theory the Order's Priories, Commanderies and Preceptories in France, Italy, Spain, Portugal, England, Scotland and Ireland, Switzerland and the German Empire were held free of rents and feudal dues. But the Knights could not escape all feudal responsibility by claiming to be religious. In Scotland the claim was never admitted, though the Order enjoyed its privileges under a series of Royal Charters.[6]

The feudal structure of Christendom was of varying complexity, and since the Order – the 'Holy Religion' as the Knights preferred to call it – had to live within that structure, their duties and their privileges (whatever Pascal II's Bull might say) varied from nation to nation. In England the feudal structure was very highly organized. This was not so in France and Spain; but everywhere a Knight owed certain duties to his immediate temporal overlord.

A large part of the income of the English Lord Prior at Clerkenwell went on the entertainment of the monarch and a horde of hungry and thirsty court officials.[7] There were 'castle guard' duties and numerous military commitments like *'fief-vente'* which were increasingly commuted into money payments. Ecclesiastical foundations in particular were permitted to commute their feudal service.[8]

'Once money replaced land as the *quid pro quo* of military service, feudalism was dead, regardless of the fact that the forms, language, and personal relationships of feudalism might linger on for centuries.'[9]

The Knights of St. John owed no national loyalty in the modern sense. The feudal duties of nobles and gentlemen might be owed to different overlords in the same country or to the same overlords in different countries. The one static and continuous factor for the Holy Religion was the Papacy as spiritual overlord. How far the overlordship of the Holy Father extended to temporal affairs was to be a source of perpetual preoccupation for both parties.

Try as they might – and we may suppose that at times they did not try very hard – the Hospitallers could not as individuals keep out of the wars of Christian against Christian, or out of national politics. The English 'Langue', to which the Scots and the Irish also belonged, was particularly troubled by squabbles. Pius II noted that 'there was nothing the Scots liked better than abuse of the English'; and the Irish, from that land where 'time had stood still, as it is apt to do for the Celts', spent much of their time resenting English nominations to their Priory.

The Grand Prior Robert Hales was Treasurer of England, and was so involved with the unpopular policies of his friend and confidant the Archbishop of Canterbury, that Wat Tyler's popular insurrection burned Clerkenwell to the ground and lynched both Archbishop and Prior in 1381. The Grand Prior Robert Botyll fought against Henry VI at Northampton; and John Langstrother, Castellan of Rhodes, who had been sent to England by the Grand Master de Lastic to seek aid from Henry VI after the fall of Constantinople in 1453, was later to become so involved in supporting Henry against Edward IV that we find him commanding the van of Queen Margaret's army, under the

Duke of Somerset, at Tewkesbury in 1471. Amongst the Knights and Squires of the Order who followed him were Sir Thomas Tressham and Sir Gervaise Colyton. After the battle, the defeated Knights took sanctuary in Tewkesbury Abbey, but they were seized and brought to trial before the Dukes of Gloucester and Norfolk. Condemned, with the Duke of Somerset and many others, for open rebellion, they were beheaded in the market place.

Sir Thomas Docwra, who narrowly missed election to the Grand Magistry of Rhodes in 1521, sat in the English parliament with precedence as the premier baron of England, and accompanied the Earl of Shrewsbury, Captain of Henry VIII's vanguard, 'upon the King's going into France in 1513'.

Scottish Knights are said to have fought on the English side at Bannockburn on the Feast of St. John, 1314, and John Sandilands died at Flodden with the 'flowers of the forest' in 1513. Nevertheless, throughout all the Anglo-Scottish wars, safe conducts were issued for any Hospitaller journeying to the Convent in Rhodes.[10]

The shape which the Order assumed in Rhodes was to remain recognizable five centuries later, and the organization of the Holy Religion does not differ, in essentials, today.

The Knights who formed the permanent fighting nucleus of the Order and occupied all the important commands, belonged to the first of the three principal classes into which the Order was divided – the Knights of Justice. They were all sons of the great houses of Europe, and had to prove noble birth on both sides of their family for something like four generations: this is a necessary over-simplification, since 'proofs' were not made easier by the different laws of heraldry and succession in different nations. The English, Italians and Spaniards demanded four quarterings, the French eight, and the Germans sixteen. Modern divisions of the Order are more complex, to meet the altered structure of society.

Novices had all to serve for two years in the Convent – the headquarters of the Order – one of which had to be served as a 'caravan' or general service commission in the galleys; after which they might return to their national Priory, Bailywick, or Commandery under the orders of their immediate superior, or perhaps be seconded to the diplomatic or military service of some prince or ecclesiastic. Many might remain in the Convent for years, or for a lifetime; but all were under strict obedience to report to the Convent when so ordered, under pain of disgrace and dismissal – perhaps excommunication – if they disobeyed. The Grand Master's executive powers were not absolute. He ruled with the consent of Council and the whole Order, and there was a system of equity whereby an aggrieved brother might appeal, through a series of appellate courts, to Rome. Plenary powers were granted in emergency – in 1480 and in 1522 – but L'Isle Adam consulted the Council before the final surrender of the city.

After the Knights of Justice came the Chaplains of Obedience, for whom there were no restrictions as to birth and whose duties were strictly religious, though many of them bore arms in emergency. The third class consisted of the Serving Brothers or Servants-at-Arms, who needed only to be 'gentlemen' and required no proof of nobility.

There was a fourth class – ranking 'with but after' the Knights of Justice, and only rarely promoted to the higher posts – known as Knights of Grace, whose personal merits were accepted in lieu of noble quarterings. Promotion from the ranks of the Serving Brothers was also possible, and the rules might always be varied by dispensation to meet emergencies or deserving cases, as with the immediate admission and promotion to Grand Cross of Gabriele Tadini in 1522. The ranks of Grand Cross, Grand Prior, Knights of Justice and of Grace, and Chaplains of Obedience – as well as the very precise rules about quarterings – belong more properly to the Malta period of the Order. In Rhodes, the practices were applied without precise definition.

By the fifteenth century the Order had been divided into the eight Tongues or Langues which tended to cut across national divisions. The term 'Langue' as a division of the Order first appears in the Statuta of Margat in 1206. These were (in 1461) in order of seniority: Provence, Auvergne, France, Italy, Aragon, England, Germany, Castile and Portugal. Each Langue was divided into a number of Priories, thus: Provence had the Priories of St. Gilles and Toulouse; Auvergne, a single Priory of Auvergne; France, those of France, Aquitaine and Champagne;

Italy, those of Rome, Lombardy, Capua, Pisa, Sicily, Barletta, Hungary and Venice; Aragon, those of Amposta, Catalonia and Navarre; England, those of Ireland and England (Scotland ranking only as a Commandery); Germany, those of Brandenburg, Bohemia and Germany; Castile and Portugal, those of Castile, Portugal and Leon.

Certain posts were reserved for the senior officer (the Pilier) of each particular Langue. The Pilier of Provence was always Grand Commander; the Pilier of Auvergne, the Marshal; of France, the Hospitaller; of Italy, the Admiral; of Aragon, the Grand Conservator; of England, the 'Turcopilier' – in effect, commander of the light cavalry. The origin of the title, sometimes appearing as 'Turcopolier' has been ascribed to the Greek 'Turcopolos', suggesting that the light cavalry were recruited, like the Janissaries, from the offspring of enemy (Muslim) parents. The Pilier of Germany was Grand Bailiff; and of Castile and Portugal, the Chancellor.

The executive government of the Order rested with the Grand Master and Council. The Council consisted of the Bishop, the Prior of the Conventual Church, the Piliers of each Langue, the Conventual Bailiffs and all Knights Grand Cross present in the Convent. The Convent could be wherever the Grand Master happened to be.

Supreme legislative authority was vested in the Chapter General over which the Grand Master presided. The Bishop of the diocese in which the Convent was located, the Grand Prior of the Conventual Church, the Conventual Bailiffs, the Priors of the Langues, and a Grand Cross from each Langue comprised the Chapter, which elected two representatives from each of the eight Langues to a law-making commission: the 'Venerandi Sedici'. The archives of the Order in the Royal Library of Valletta contain surviving records of fourteen Chapters General between 1332 and 1514. At least forty were held in Rhodes. In the Holy Land, Chapters General were held every three or five years.

The election of the Grand Master – from the ranks of Knights of Justice only, and, in practice, almost always from those of the Grand Priors – was a complex affair. Only Knights of Justice of thirteen years seniority, of which three must have been spent in the Convent and three in caravans with the fleet, were entitled to a full vote. A debt of more than ten scudi to the Treasury disqualified. Conventual Chaplains and Serving Brothers were entitled to vote only in their own Langue. The election had three stages: first, twenty-four electors were named by the Langues, thereafter called the 'Conclave'. Secondly, three electors were named by the Conclave – one Knight, one Serving Brother and one Chaplain. This triumvirate then named a fourth elector. The four then proceeded to co-opt a fifth; the five a sixth, and so on until a total of sixteen was reached. The sixteen then elected a Grand Master. The casting vote (which seems to have been exercised with surprising frequency) lay with the single Knight elected initially to the Conclave.[11]

The heavy preponderance of French influence, resulting in the election of eight French Grand Masters amongst a total of eleven in the two centuries from 1305 to the loss of Rhodes, might be expected to produce a coincidence of policy between France and the Order. It is much to the credit of the French Masters and of the Piliers of the French-speaking Priories that this was so infrequently the case.

The Order's foreign policy was simple in principle – the incessant castigation of Islam; but it was less simple in execution. The Knights could not by themselves sustain a constant war against Egypt, the Emirs of Asia Minor and, as that power grew, the Ottoman Turks, as well as keeping a wary eye on the Venetians and the dying Empire of Byzantium, as long as any strength remained to it. (The Eastern Emperor had never recognized their sovereignty of Rhodes.) Thus they were driven to a series of shifts and pacts designed to prevent Islam from uniting against them. Thus, too, it was necessary to operate a complex and widespread diplomatic and intelligence service on both sides of the 'Islamic curtain'. There have always been renegades and adventurers in plenty in the Middle East, willing and anxious to spy for a good paymaster. The Order's espionage system was proverbially efficient, but it cost gold.

If Rhodes was to survive, the Priories and Commanderies had to be efficiently and lucratively 'farmed', and the prompt payment of the national taxes called 'responsions' ensured. Fortunately, the Order's aristocratic and ecclesiastic connections furnished a ready-made network of courtiers and agents throughout Europe.

Nevertheless, the responsions were not always forthcoming and the demands of the Papacy and of the new nationalisms made ever-increasing inroads into the sources of revenue – and the network itself was expensive. A constant source of friction was the Papacy's tendency to assert its overlordship by awarding benefices of the Order to its relatives and clients, few of whom could or would make any practical contribution to the Order's struggle.

Rhodes (like many other contemporary states) was a slave-owning, slave-trading society; but slaves had to be housed and, if they were to be of any use, well fed and well cared for.

Despite the manifold difficulties, we have only to recall a few of the Holy Religion's battle honours during the fourteenth and early fifteenth centuries[12] to rebut the charges of Sanudo and Piloti and the disingenuous attacks of the Avignon Papacy.

In 1312 the Order's galleys destroyed a Turkish force of twenty-three ships off Amorgos. In the same year, the galleys, allied with the Cypriots, defeated an Ottoman fleet at Ephesus. In 1334 the Order, in alliance with France and Venice, routed a Turkish fleet off Smyrna, and ten years later led the fleet of the Holy League, capturing Smyrna, which was to be occupied and held by the Knights until its fall to the Tartar Timur the Lame in 1402. 1347 brought a crushing Turkish defeat off Imbros, and in 1361 four galleys of the Order shared the victory of King Peter I of Cyprus at Adelia (or Satalia). In 1365 Alexandria was invested, captured and sacked – an expedition in which the Order played a key part.

In 1367 the whole Syrian littoral was attacked and looted from Tripoli to Alexandretta. In 1396 came the gallant failure at Nicopolis on the Danube, led by the Grand Master D'Heredia, who had fought against the English at Creçy.

In 1403 a notable treaty was achieved with the Mamelukes whereby the Order was to maintain consulates in Jerusalem, Ramleh and Damietta and to be allowed to rebuild the Hospital in Jerusalem. The Order's Rhodian subjects were also to enjoy preferential trading rights in Alexandria, Damietta, Jaffa, Beirut, Tripoli and Damascus. This excellent truce lasted until 1440, when the Mamelukes attacked Castellorizon. Four ships and eight galleys confronted an Egyptian blockading force of seventeen ships, capturing twelve and landing a body of Knights on the mainland who then slew 700 Mamelukes. In the same year a half-hearted attempt on Rhodes was repelled by the fleet.

In 1444 the Egyptians again attacked Rhodes itself; but an abortive siege lasting forty days ended with a sea battle in which the Order was victorious.

There were certainly periods of military inactivity; but the existence of the Convent itself, and the splendid Hospital in Rhodes – where the Knights themselves tended the sick poor and served their meals in utensils of gold and silver – as well as of the numerous hospitals and poor-houses everywhere in the national Priories, complied with the Holy Religion's original duty of serving the poor of Christ.

Piloti takes a characteristically Venetian view of the Hospital. The Order, he says, by forbidding the export or re-export of ship-building timber to the Muslim states had 'impoverished many merchants who were then permitted to end their days in the magnificent Hospital at Rhodes. . . .'

After the repulse of the Mameluke attack in 1444, which co-incided with Hunyadi's defeat at Varna, the pendulum of European opinion began to swing in the opposite direction towards a complacent myth of the invincibility of the Hospitallers, and a wishful conviction that they were under special divine protection, thus relieving other Christians from the tedious necessity for doing anything themselves – an attitude perhaps more dangerous than the former charges of sloth.

2

RHODES OF THE KNIGHTS

'Nísos Ródhos,' says the *Mediterranean Pilot*, '. . . is the principal island of the Dodecanese. Mount Ataviros (or Attayaro), the summit, attains a height of 3,986 feet on the western side, four miles inland. From Ataviros, the heights decrease towards the city of Ródhos, which stands at the north-eastern end of the island. The mountains are well wooded; numerous streams, mostly dry in summer, flow through the level land towards the coast. The island produces cereals, vegetables, limes, oranges, lemons and other fruits. Sponges and fish are obtained from the surrounding waters. The island possesses an agreeable healthy climate; during summer vessels may anchor in safety off the south-eastern coast. In winter, in the cloudy and thick weather with southerly winds, great caution is required when navigating the channel between Nísos Ródhos and the coast of Asia Minor. . . .'[1]

A not unattractive picture, even in the matter-of-fact language of the *Pilot*.

By sea Rhodes lies about 600 miles from Constantinople, 360 from Alexandria, 270 from Athens, 300 from Famagusta in Cyprus, 200 from Candia in Crete, and 1,400 from Marseilles. For a vessel under sails and oars, making good perhaps five knots, the passage from Marseilles would occupy some twelve days. Crete and Cyprus were within two to three days. But the passage from the excellent Turkish anchorage at Physcos, or Marmarice, was only four hours, and much less with a 'soldier's wind'.

The wind and the weather generally favoured the oar-powered galley over short passages against the ship relying on her sails. In July and August the Etesians blow with the regularity of a trade wind from the north-west, and these would carry reinforcements, munitions and victuals from Europe to Rhodes with ease and in relative safety; but the light, variable winds of May and June would delay such passages, and the south-easterly gales of January and February and the north-easterlies of November and

December would deter all but the hardiest of seamen from navigating the waters of Rhodes with their shoals, rocks and currents, and winter mists.

From June to August Rhodes is practically rainless; but from November to January hail and rain storms are common, the temperature falls from the summer eighties to the damp and chilling fifties, and night frosts are usual: ideal conditions for breeding fevers and scurvy amongst galley slaves and armies in the field.

The island is shaped like some amphibious monster with the sharp snout of Kum Burnu (Akra Milos, or Capo della Sabbia) pointing north-east towards Cape Marmarice and the Latmus mountains of the Asian mainland, and the two flippers of the Monolithos and Lindos promontories on the west and eastward flanks, two-thirds of the way towards the monster's tail at Cape Prasonisi. From snout to tail the distance, as the crow flies, is about forty miles and the girth at its broadest is twenty miles.

The south-west coast is without a secure anchorage for vessels of any considerable draught. The wide bay of Apolakia is open to west or southerly winds. High cliffs, with small, sandy bays follow as far as Cape Kopria. Here, to the eastward, is the small, ancient port of Skala Kamirou (ancient Kamiros or Langonia); and to the north, within four miles of Kum Burnu, is the entrance point of the Bay of Trianda. The coast is high and rocky where the north-western slopes of Mount St. Stephen come right down to the sea; but farther northwards the land is low and sandy and there are good shingle beaches. Landing is not difficult and there are streams of fresh water.

Mount St. Stephen, known to the Rhodians as 'Monte Smith' since Sir William Sidney Smith made his headquarters there during his campaign against Napoleon, overlooks the city and port of Rhodes, and has, on its summit, near the remains of the ancient stadium and the temple of Apollo, a signal station exactly where its ancestor stood in 1480.

To the south-west of the village of Trianda stands the 'remarkable, solitary, rectangular shaped peak of Oros Phileremos'[2] a name which has passed into history as the sacred, mystic mountain of the Knights Hospitallers, who still invoke the intercession of Our Lady of Phileremos.

On the south-eastern coast there are several small bays, albeit guarded by rocky hazards, as far as Lardos Bay and Port Lindos at the foot of Mount Lindos, whence, near the ancient acropolis of Athena Lindia, 1,500 feet high, the noble ruins of the Knights' impregnable castle still look down.

There are adequate anchorages in the Bays of Viglika and Malona, but with shoals and rocks. The Bay of Aphandos has a sandy beach, and the northern part of Kalitheas is a secure anchorage, clear of dangers, in the summer months. The northern extremity of Kalitheas Bay is Cape Voudhi (Vudhi) between which and Kum Burnu lies the Bay of Acandia and the port of Rhodes. From westward of Cape Voudhi the land slopes gently down to the city. Kum Burnu is low and sandy, and landing is possible on either side of it in good weather. In the summer months the currents around Kum Burnu set towards the Cape – in winter, away from it.

The port of Rhodes has consisted since classical times of two artificial harbours. The 'Porto del Mandraccio' or Galley Port, the northern of the two, is entered between Lazaretto (or Posillipo) Point, about four cables south-eastward of Kum Burnu, and the extremity of the ancient mole, which extends northwards from the coast. The entrance is about one cable (600 feet) wide. The massive bulk of the Tower of St. Nicholas, close to which is the site of the Colossus, still stands on the outer end of the mole. The 'Porto Mercantile' or Commercial Port is the southern of the two artificial harbours and is protected to the eastward by a mole, extending northward from the city, upon which stands the Tower of St. Angelo. A tranverse mole, on the extremity of which stood the Tower of Grand Master Naillac (since called the Arabs' Tower) extends eastwards from the northern end of the city towards the head of the eastern mole. The entrance is little more than a cable wide. To the south-eastward is the Bay of Acandia.

Inland, Rhodes is a complex of hills and mountains and table-lands, rising to several considerable peaks, separated by hundreds of water-courses and ravines. There are pine forests, planes and oaks, wild pomegranates, cypress and fig. Five centuries ago it is likely that the forests were even more extensive, and the wild life more various. It still includes badgers, martens, weasels, hares, rabbits, foxes, partridges, eagles and falcons.[3] We are told that the Knights hunted and were guilty of extravagance and vanity in the breeding of their hounds and their falcons.

The early years of the Order's sovereignty saw a hunt of a peculiar kind. There was, it seems, a fearsome dragon who had established himself in the ravine of Santrouli on the southern slopes of Mount St. Stephen, whence he preyed upon the defence-less peasantry, devouring in particular the nubile Rhodian maidens. A number of Knights had lost their lives in combat with the dragon, and the Grand Master had forbidden further opera-tions against him; but one Dieudonné de Gozon, a Provençal, combining artifice with gallantry, having 'trained a team of English bulldogs to attack a wooden model of the beast' (accord-ing to a legend repeated by Porter),[4] disobeyed and destroyed the dragon. He was deprived of his habit for disobedience; but in response to popular clamour he was reinstated and rose to be Grand Master himself, ruling from 1346 to 1353.

Whatever the true nature of the dragon, it does seem that de Gozon slew some predatory beast out of the run of the normal fauna, to the delight of the Rhodian peasantry. The archives of the Order invariably dub him 'Extinctor Draconis', and the poet Schiller celebrated the legend in his epic *Der Kampf mit dem Drachen*. We ought, perhaps, to forget the English bulldogs, though even they are not impossible.

Rhodes – *Heliousa*, the Sun Friend – is very lovely. Her long valleys are rich and green with daphne and myrtle and wild almond and oleander; and the ravine of Petaloudes where, from June to September, 'the butterflies seem like specks of fire in the aquarium light beneath the leaves',[5] was famous centuries before the Hospitallers. The hillsides are bright with anemones in spring and cyclamen in the autumn, and wild orchis and asphodel and sand lilies by the seashore. In summer the blue of the 'maned Aegean' is indescribable.

In the gently rolling country to the west and north of the forti-fied city the Knights had their villas, their farms and their gardens, where they bred livestock and cultivated apricots, oranges, figs, lemons and grapes, and spent their brief hours of ease. The sunsets are fantastic. The purple nights are long and full of stars. Amongst the orange groves and the vines, when the west wind blew the scent of the pines and the wild thyme down from the Nereid-haunted hills and some native Linus plucked out an ancient air on his lute, it may not have been too difficult for the young Knight to forget the fields of Auvergne or the bluebells of the English woodland. To the east loomed the gaunt mountains of Caria on the Turkish mainland, whence death might come with the dawn; but the young Knight could say with St. Francis:

Laudato si', mi Signore,
per sora luna e le stelle
in celu l'ai formata clarite
et pretiose et belle.

Laudato si', mi Signore, per
sora nostra morte corporale
da quale nullu homo vivente
o scappare . . .

Be praised, my Lord, for
Sister Moon and the stars,
in heaven you have made them
clear and precious and lovely

Be praised, my Lord, for our
Sister Bodily Death, from whom
no living man may escape. . . .

At the time of the fall of Constantinople in 1453, Rhodes was a typical walled city of its time, somewhat more heavily fortified than most, disposed in a rough semi-circle about the commercial port. Every exertion had been used, within the Order's resources, to keep the defences up to date; but the development of siege cannon had been too rapid and Rhodes still presented essentially the old pre-gunpowder arrangement of high, thin walls, and towers and ditches. There were no bastions to provide flanking fire against breaches in the walls, which were to become commoner than the old, suicidal scaling attacks; and the towers and walls were still embellished with obsolescent machicolations and *hourds*, or timber pent-houses, designed for the long bow and

33

boiling oil. The general lay-out of the city also had about it something of the ancient donjon-and-keep arrangement of the earlier crusading castles, with gateways guarded by round towers, drawbridge and portcullis; there were *aleoirs*, or walk-ways connecting the towers, and curtain walls of revetments filled with rubble, as high as they could be made.

To the north, facing towards the galley port, was the 'Collachio', or Convent proper, which housed the Knights, the Grand Master's palace, the Hospital and all the administrative buildings of the Holy Religion, as well as the Conventual Church of St. John the Baptist, Patron and Protector of the Order. The Collachio was separated from the town by a wall, with watch-towers and two gateways. The Merchants' Quarter or 'Borgo' was a well laid-out city of palaces and grand houses, with a piazza communicating with the 'Marina' or commercial quays. It occupied rather more than a half the total area of the city to the south and west of the Convent. The south-eastern section of the semi-circle was the Jews' Quarter, or Ghetto.

Each section of the city's enceinte with its thirteen towers was allocated to a Langue. Thus, France held the northern approach, with Germany next, on the western flank: Auvergne and Aragon followed to the south-west; England held the southernmost sector, with Provence on her eastern flank; while Italy and Castile shared the seaward approaches. The harbours were protected by the Towers of Naillac (1396) on the extremity of the short mole of the commercial port and of St. John (or St. Angelo) on its longer mole (1346).

After the fall of Constantinople, the Grand Master de Lastic called in Florentine experts to strengthen and modernize the defences. They doubled the enceinte by adding a second series of curtains and ramparts, and deepening and widening the ditch. In 1461 the Grand Master Zacosta completed the Tower of St. Nicholas on the extremity of the mole of the galley port.

The city had one serious weakness; the countryside outside the walls and beyond the counterscarp of the ditch was, according to Marie Dupuis,[6] a French Knight, 'the most admirable country in the world for carrying on a siege, for all around there were numerous gardens filled with little churches and Greek chapels, with odd walls and stones, and rocks behind which cover could always be found against the garrison, to such an extent that if all the artillery in the world had been inside the town, it could do no harm to those that were without, provided they did not approach too close.'

Throughout the island the Order had erected, or restored, some thirty castles and strong points: notably at Villa Nuova, Kopria, Langonia, Monolithos, Asklepion, Lardos, Lindos, Malona, Feracle (Pheraclos or Pheraclyea) and Archangelos. There were few roads, though plenty of cart-tracks and bridle-paths, and communications seem to have been remarkably good. Watch-towers around the whole coastline were kept manned. A primitive semaphore and carrier pigeons by day, and signal fires by night, ensured that alarms reached the Convent rapidly.

The outlying islands each had their garrison and at least one dispatch vessel, though the galley squadron or some allied privateers might operate from any of them as the *guerre de course* demanded.

On the mainland, near Halicarnassos, the Holy Religion still held its great fortress of Budrum, or St. Peter, captured by the Knights during the temporary eclipse of Ottoman power by the Tartar Timur Lenk, and built with the stones of the Mausoleum. At Budrum the arms of the princes who subscribed towards the cost of erecting the fortress may still be discerned. They include those of King Henry IV of England, and of the Dukes of Clarence, Bedford, York and Gloucester.

The Rhodians were generally loyal to the Order; but they were proud of their ancient traditions: of Dorian Hexapolis with its colonies at Parthenope (Naples), and as far afield as France and Spain; of ancient Lindos with nine ships at the siege of Troy, and they did not enjoy their position under the Order as second-class citizens.

Vertot is uncomplimentary about the Rhodian lower classes: 'they were . . .' he says, 'insensible to any passion but fear, and could never be brought to look danger in the face' – a judgement which is scarcely consistent with the evidence. The Rhodians are justly proud of a long history of courage and sturdy independence. The Greeks had a word for their fame as seamen: 'Ten Rhodians: ten ships.' They were no strangers to siege. In 304 B.C. they beat off Demetrius Poliocetes. Their city was sacked by

Mithridates and gutted by Cassius. Rhodian learning, too, was pre-eminent in the classical world. Cicero, Brutus and Cassius attended the school of oratory in Rhodes.

But a great part of the subjects of the Holy Religion were not native Rhodians. Local society was a 'Latin-Greek amalgam characteristic of the Western Colonies in the Aegean (like Crete and Chios). The city of Rhodes was dominated by an indispensible colonist element of merchants, bankers, ship-builders, architects, engineers, lawyers and craftsmen who had immigrated from Spain, Italy and France and in some instances from as far afield as Germany and England. These settlers were not themselves members of the Order, but its lay subjects who brought out wives from the West and founded families at Rhodes. At all times they were a minority, outnumbered by the indigenous Greeks, who formed the peasant and artisan classes and were firmly restricted to subordinate roles under Hospitaller rule.'[7]

The Greek Rhodians had no political power and were rarely amongst the wealthier merchants. Porter has a word of praise for the manner in which Greek and Latin Christians co-existed and fought side by side against the Muslim: 'When we consider,' he says, 'that the population of Rhodes all professed the Greek faith, it is a matter of wonder that they should have remained loyal under the sway of an Order so eminently Roman Catholic as that of the Hospital. Either the differences and jealousies between the rival creeds must in those days have been far less embittered than in later years, or the Order must have learnt a lesson in religious toleration such as the professors of their faith have never been celebrated for practising . . .'[8]

We may pass over Porter's Victorian reference to Catholic intolerance. He was writing in Malta at a time when relations between the established Catholic Church and the English Protestants were bad. Unhappily, he is wrong about the Rhodians. They had little choice. Their Patriarch and their parish clergy were appointed by the Grand Master from the ranks of those Orthodox clergy who recognized the Emperor Constantine XI's Decree of 'Henotikon', and were, in the light of the Council of Florence, what we now call Catholics of the Greek Rite, owing allegiance to the Pope of Rome and not to the Patriarch of Constantinople.

It is clear that there was no overt schism between Greeks and

Latins. The Augustinian Friar Giacomo de Curti tells us how Knights and people prayed and received the sacraments together in churches of both rites, invoked the aid of the same saints and venerated the same relics. There were, nevertheless, some Rhodians who 'preferred the turban to the Latin mitre'.

On 29th May 1453 Constantinople fell. Mehmet the Conqueror lost no time in demanding tribute from the Holy Religion. It was – and he knew it – unthinkable.

On 20th January 1454, the Grand Master Jean de Lastic wrote to his confrere, the Prior of Auvergne:

> Shall we stand, then, like poor sheep surrounded by wolves and other ferocious beasts? To expect succour from our Christian neighbours is vain, for they stand in the same danger as we ourselves. To expect it from the Christians of the West? It is to be feared that it will not come, or, if it comes that it will be too late. Counting on nobody but ourselves, our Brethren and our Subjects, we urge you by the Passion of Our Lord and Saviour Jesus Christ, indeed, we command you in virtue of your Holy Obedience . . . to come with all possible speed to the Convent. . . . Hasten![9]

But no great attack came.

In 1457, attacks on Kos, Symi and Nisyros were beaten off; but the Order's fleet did not save Lemnos, Thasos or Lesbos. A landing in the Bay of Malona had some small success, the Ottomans sacking the castles of Malona and Archangelos before they were driven back to the sea; but for the next twenty-three years Mehmet was busy consolidating his frontiers to the north and the east, and the Order was able to take and to hold the initiative at sea.

3

MEN AND WEAPONS

The image of the crusader clothed in mail and emblazoned surcoat, mounted on a charger as splendidly caparisoned as his rider, pricking through the glades of Gramarye towards the Holy Land with nodding panache and fluttering pennoncel was never quite true, and the lives and manners of the last of the crusaders in Rhodes at the turn of the fifteenth century had little in common with romantic notions of what chivalry ought to be like or with the tilt-yards and tourneys of their homelands. The older Knights of 1480, it is true, had grown up in a Europe where only the beginnings of the revolutionary changes in the art of war (and politics) were being felt. Scions of noble houses whose trade was fighting, they had been nurtured in the old traditions of hard exercise at the 'quintain' – a stout wooden dummy Saracen at which the young mounted esquires aimed their strokes with two-handed sword, mace, axe, lance and short pike, like schoolboys at the cricket nets – of falconry, hunting, duelling, catechism and a little book-learning in monkish Latin. Most could read in the vernacular, but writing was not a knightly accomplishment. Yet some Knights – the Grand Master d'Aubusson is a notable example – were men of wide culture, well read in the Greek and Latin classics and in the growing literature of the Renaissance; linguists and accomplished diplomats, who were thoroughly informed of every technical advance in the art of war.

By 1522, more than a generation later, the technical revolution, largely brought about by the invention of gunpowder and the rapid development of the cannon and the 'hand-gun', was almost complete, and the Knights of the Holy Religion had shown themselves remarkably adaptable to it. Knights like L'Isle Adam, William Weston and D'Amaral were reading the new printed works of Machiavelli and Guicciardini, and the *Nef des Princes* of Robert de Balsac with its study of siege work. They had long since abandoned the false pride of a Bayard who could complain (in 1509) that the Emperor ought not to 'peril so much nobleness together with his infantry, of whom one is a shoe-maker, another a farrier, another a baker, and suchlike mechanics, who hold not their honour as do we gentlemen'.[1] Neither did the Servants-at-Arms insist, like the French and German men-at-arms before Padua, that they were 'not such as went on foot, nor to go into a breach, their true estate being to fight like gentlemen on horse-back'.[2]

The Order's taking to the sea had had something to do with this valuable lesson in humility. On shipboard, the Knights had learned that – in battle at least – it was essential to be 'all of one company'.

Life in the Convent was pleasant enough, if not quite as luxurious and licentious as the Order's critics made out. Each Langue had its own 'Auberge' or Inn (still to be seen in the Street of the Knights), where the younger Knights lived a firmly disciplined, communal life, under the command of their Conventual Pilier or Grand Cross, feeding together in their mess and performing their regular watches and turns of duty in the Hospital, about the defences and in the galley port; attending Holy Mass and the prescribed offices of the Order daily. Once fully trained, and having served their required commission in the galleys, they would be selected for detached duty in the garrisons of the outlying islands, or to man the coastguard posts, or the strong-points in the countryside of Rhodes, or at St. Peter on the mainland.

Outside the Convent, in the city, the young Knights were required by their Rule to go 'in twos or threes and not according to their choice; but with those whom the Master has ordered'; and they must allow 'nothing in their dress or their actions which might offend the eye of anyone, but only what is suitable to their sacred vocation'.[3] No woman might wash their heads or their feet or make their beds. In no case might their clothing be made of fur. They were to eat only twice a day; and on the fourth day of the week and 'on the Sabbath, that is Saturday, and also from Septuagesima to Easter, let them not eat meat, except those who are ill or weak; and let them never sleep naked, but dressed in woollen or linen shirts, or in other similar garments'.

As to fornication, the Rule imposed a curious sanction: 'If a

Brother – may that never happen! – fall into fornication because of the strength of evil passions, if he has sinned in secret, let him repent in secret and impose on himself a suitable penance.'[4] If, on the other hand, his sin were 'known and proved', a cleric was to be beaten by his superior and a layman 'beaten very severely with whips and sticks' and excluded from the Order, only to be re-admitted after suitable penances and a year's probation.

But there were also feast days and holidays when the Knights were free to indulge in those gargantuan fifteen-course meals of which we read:[5] venison with hot pepper sauce; wild boar with spices; bear; peacocks and swans; fowls, and capons with cloves and garlic; hare and rabbit; crane, heron, plover and mallard; pasties of venison, pigeons and pheasants; bird pies; and fish – Mediterranean mullet, tuna, mackerel, swordfish, dentici, shellfish and young squids. For fruit there were figs, apples, muscatels, limes, lemons and oranges, and there was cheese and plenty of the heavy, crusty Mediterranean bread, dusted with sesame seed.

They imported Cretan and their own Cypriot wines, and there was Rhodian wine, all heavily laced with spices. The ships from Europe would bring in French, Italian, Spanish and German wines, and there was a regular tribute of salmon[6] from Scotland.

The fifteenth-century table was far from rugged, and the Auberges of the Convent maintained a civilized standard. An inventory of some of the possessions of the English Auberge, one of the least rich, shortly after the retreat from Rhodes, included 'a parcel of silver bearing the arms of Darrel, Boswell, Lancelot, Pemberton and Barnaby, as well as those of Weston . . . including pitchers, basins, trenchers and spoons . . . tablecloths, towels and little napkins of diaper . . . porringers, saucers and wine pots'.

On feast days, there were tournaments and regattas, horse racing and religious processions for Knights and people alike. In their off-duty hours the young men could play chess and backgammon, or listen to music on lutes, psalteries, viols and the portable organ; and there was always plenty of exercise – falconry and hunting, and (although strictly forbidden by the Master) duelling.[7]

Life in the smaller galleys was tough: 'They were overcrowded with slave oarsmen, fighting men and crew, cumbered with arms and provisions, so that it was often impossible to lie down to sleep. There was neither shade from the blazing sun nor shelter from rain and sea water. Swept by sudden storms, the food would become sodden, useless, the men sick or fever-struck. After a successful encounter, the galleys would be still more overcrowded with captives and booty.'[8]

And it was little better in the 'great ships', with their added unpleasantness of stinking, disease-breeding bilges. But there was another side to the picture. The great two-decker galleys were supplied with awnings, and the *Libri Bullarum* of the Order show considerate, even paternal care for the galley slaves; and from 1250 onwards the Order, like the Genoese, Venetians and Catalans, had their shipping regulations which called for high standards of sanitation, fire precautions, accommodation and habitability.

The Holy Religion was never able, alone, to mount full-scale pitched battles or prolonged sieges, on the pattern of the Italian wars of France and Spain. Its function was a sustained *guerre de course* against Muslim shipping (and that of its European collaborators), and to be prepared, always, to repel Turkish and Mameluke attacks on the outposts and on the Convent itself. And to this end, its recruiting, training and equipment were a modified version of contemporary practice. Cavalry, for example, still a main arm of the major European powers, was little more than a ceremonial anachronism. Since there was, as yet, no 'naval' warfare, but only land-fighting transferred afloat, there were few differences in the manning of land and sea forces. The fighting galleys – in effect the successors of the Order's cavalry arm – adopted cavalry tactics, advancing upon the enemy in line abreast, the weather gauge mattering little to these primarily oar-propelled vessels. They mounted one or more small and not very effective cannon in the bows, where there was also a fighting platform upon which the Knights were drawn up in battle order, supported by cross-bowmen and arquebusiers in the rear ranks. The object was to ram and board, and the outcome depended more on brute force and determination in hand-to-hand combat than on any special skill. The really vital missile weapons were the cross-bow and the short-bow, although after 1359 cannon began to develop an effective role at sea in shooting down masts and rigging, superstructures and crew. The high freeboard of the larger, mainly cargo-carrying carracks of the Ottomans and the Egyptians presented little difficulty. The old land siege methods of scaling the ship's side with the aid of hook ropes was effective. The ropes were difficult to cast off once they had taken the strain of one or two armoured assailants, and a man leaning over the bulwarks to cut them could be picked off with an arquebus from below.

The sea combat structure of the Order's fighting power was well adapted to siege conditions. The galley slaves could be disembarked and used as pioneers and sappers – under surveillance. The *forzati*, or pressed men, and the gentlemen volunteers or *buonavoglie*, who were mostly seamen by trade or inclination, could be most useful in a number of ways calling for skill with ropes and tackles, like the handling of heavy masonry or the transport of cumbersome artillery, the improvisation of palisades or earthworks. Then there were the mercenaries, recruited for their special weapon skills: arquebusiers from Spain and Italy, pikemen from Switzerland, cross-bowmen from Brabant, and Welsh and English long-bowmen. There were also the locally raised militia – conscripts, but paid for their 'servitus marinarie' from the proceeds of the mill tax.

Gunners were harder to come by, the new science of gunnery requiring a high degree of expertise and some scientific education. The best artillery experts were from France and Germany, and the master gunners were rare and expensive.

The Knights themselves did not readily take to gunpowder, that

> . . . base implement of Death
> Framed in the black Tartarean
>   realms,
> By Beelzebub's malicious art
>   beneath designed
> To ruin all the race of humankind

– as Ariosto wrote.

Although they made full and efficient use of artillery in their defence of Rhodes, and the gun-port is said to have been invented there, there was still some feeling that it was ungentlemanly, even against unbelievers, and the Grand Master had some difficulty in restraining hot-headed defenders from the more gentlemanly tactic of mounted sorties.

The Egyptians had relegated gunpowder, whose use had been forbidden against fellow Muslim by the Caliph, to their Negro militia. They complained that Ottoman victories had been won by its aid.

The time of change from 1480 to 1522 opened with a bewildering variety of old and new weapons. The long-bow, of Welsh origin, which could discharge six aimed shots a minute with a range of 340 yards,[9] and whose arrow could pierce a one-inch board at the end of its flight, was still in use, as was the cross-bow, or miniature arbalest, which fired an armour-penetrating bolt (at much shorter range). The cross-bow had been outlawed (with little effect) from use against Christians by the Lateran Council in 1139. The cross-bow also had a special value in its high trajectory. It could be fired to descend vertically over walls and the heads of troops. Then there was the Turkish composite, or double bow, of immense power, and a selection of long and short pikes, halberds and bills sufficient to satisfy the most blood-thirsty imagination. They included the English bill and the 'glaive', designed to unhorse and dismember armoured cavalry, and looking remarkably like a giant tin-opener; the scythe-like 'guisarme' and the crescent-bladed half-axe, half-pike which the Flemings called a 'good morning'. There was also the spiked mace called by the Germans a 'morning star'. But the favourite weapon of the Knight remained the heavy, two-handed sword with its double, biting, crushing edge; and, for his opponent the Janissary, the long, curved scimitar with a single, fine cutting edge.

Amongst a variety of not very efficient hand-guns the arquebus was the least inefficient; but its earlier versions took as long to load and fire a single round as it took a long-bowman to fire six aimed arrows; and it required three yards of cotton cord, soaked in saltpetre, as its fuse. Kept smouldering at night, the fuse gave away the position of the arquebusiers. The arquebus could only be aimed with the aid of a rest, and like all early fire-arms it was apt to be useless in wet weather.

But the hand-gun and the cannon had come to stay. The very heavy pieces, like the massive freak used against Constantinople in 1453 – a bronze breech-loader from the Adrianople foundry of

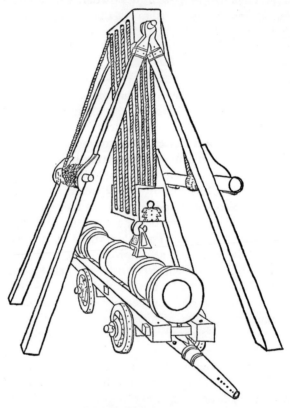

A large bombard on its carriage

the renegade Hungarian Master Urbanus, weighing over seventeen tons, with a casing five and a half inches thick, and casting a great stone ball over a range of a mile – or the larger mortars which fired shot weighing 250 lb, could not be transported to Rhodes without disproportionate expenditure of men and treasure. In 1480 most artillery was still lashed to wooden beds with hemp, and the larger pieces were incapable of being elevated or depressed. The Turkish siege guns at Rhodes fired stone balls at useful ranges up to 500 yards. They seemed chiefly to have been basilisks, serpentines and culverins, bombards and mortars. By 1522 iron balls were in use, except by the short range cannon perrier; and there were port pieces, fitted with wheels, and the newly invented trunnion, and the delightfully named 'murthering pieces', which fired leaden bullets and short lengths of iron bar. Rifling of gun barrels appeared in 1520, though judging from the ranges used there were no rifled guns at Rhodes. There were no more huge pieces with screwed-in breeches which could fire only a few times a day. Long guns with a very wide bore had been abandoned in favour of portability and accuracy, and the newer weapons could be shifted about with relative ease in the course of a battle or siege. Against masonry the guns were very effective, though less certain against men unless they advanced – as did the Turks – in compact, close formations.

By 1522 portable fire-arms had improved too. The useful range of the arquebus was 400 yards and the new matchlock enabled the marksman to use both hands to steady his weapon and to concentrate on his aim, undistracted by the match.[10]

Siege weapons included the ancient 'Greek fire' – a compound of quicklime, some form of petroleum and sulphur, ignited by adding water to the quicklime and syphoned upon the besiegers in a stream of liquid fire. The *trebuchet* – whose last recorded use was at Rhodes in 1480 – was a great wooden engine which projected a huge rock from the free and longer end of a revolving arm whose motive power was provided by a counter-weight at the shorter end. The *mangonel*, with a spoon-shaped arm operated by a windlass, could be used for hurling jars of 'wild fire' or *carcasses* – clay 'eggs' filled with a burning mixture of pitch, pinewood, charcoal and tow, which burst on impact and could only be extinguished with vinegar, urine or glue. Both trebuchet and mangonel could be used to hurl the rotting corpses of men and horses into a besieged town – an early form of chemical warfare.

The laborious and hazardous business of undermining walls and underpinning the foundations with baulks of timber which were then set alight, cracking and collapsing the masonry, or of effecting a breach by the use of rams and bores, was still more effective in 1480 than gunfire; but by 1522 the explosive mine had proved better than either, and the Ottomans, who were always ready to profit from the experience of the Christians in their Italian wars, made full use of the new weapon against Rhodes. In the event, despite the valiant countermining of Tadini da Martinengo, the gunpowder mine was the decisive

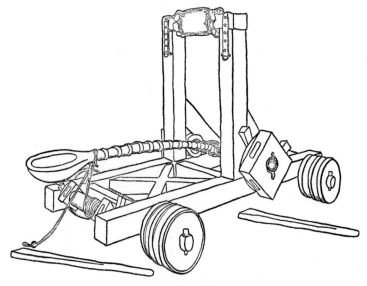

A mangonel in the loading position

weapon. First used in 1487 by the Genoese against the Florentine castle of Serezanella, it was not very successful, most of the charges exploding ineffectually or in the wrong places. The Spaniards were more fortunate against Naples in 1503, when they destroyed a section of the wall of the Castel d'Ovo, compelling its surrender. As with other renaissance weapons, the techniques needed for maximum effectiveness were beyond the mathematics of the sixteenth century – Turkish or Christian. The essentials were to secure the galleries and chambers against collapse by means of props and shores at the correct intervals; to position the mine in the right spot; and, most important, to know the proper charge of powder, which varied with the nature of the rock or soil, to give the desired effect at various depths.

Accurate calculation of distance, depth and direction, short of physical measurement and trial and error, depended on trigonometry or, at its most elementary, on algebra. In the application of this (Muslim) science to the art of war both the Ottomans and the Europeans seem to have been slow. Perhaps the Turks knew how to use triangulation for ascertaining the required length and bearing of their galleries; though Regiomontanus did not publish his work on the relationship of the sides of triangles to the sines of their corresponding angles until 1533 (in Nuremberg).[11] Perhaps Suleiman's spies had furnished sufficiently accurate plans of Rhodes to make these calculations easier; but, even over the short distance from counterscarp to bastion, there was still some tricky subterranean navigation to be done with mason's level and simple magnetic needle.

Mathematics were also needed to decide the quantity of powder required to 'lift' an estimated weight of soil, rock and masonry from a known depth along the line of least resistance to the explosion. Eighteenth-century British and French sappers were still arguing about the proper formula,[12] so it is little wonder that the Turkish operations in 1522 were wasteful of lives and powder.

The principles of countermining were well understood:

> A miner that knows how to use counter-mines constructed as they ought to be, may stop the enemy miners, stifle them or destroy them or destroy their works in such a manner as to make it impossible for others to return to the same place, or if he please let them enter the galleries, block up the passages and take them prisoner, or kill them if thought proper. . . .[13]

But the intelligence that Suleiman intended to reduce Rhodes by mining came too late for the defenders, advised by Tadini, to construct a proper system of countermining defences. Tadini had to assess, as exactly as possible, the depth and direction of the enemy's gallery, to drive his tunnel under it and place his own charge so that it would destroy the enemy's works, and bury his miners, at a point which would not do the Muslim's work for them by damaging the defences. His invention of a stressed parchment diaphragm which caused small, finely mounted bells to tinkle at any subterranean vibration, and his painstaking practice in using this device and training others to use it, certainly simplified his problem. Previously, the primitive, ear-to-ground method was the only possible warning, and it cannot have been very accurate, since it relied on the acuteness of individual hearing and individual judgement. But Tadini's rudimentary 'sonar' also required such judgement; and contemporaries were impressed by his magic. If the somewhat sketchy descriptions by Bourbon and Pantaleone have been properly understood, Tadini was ahead of his time, too, in developing a system of 'vents' – virtually perforating his own fortifications with the object of dispersing the blast of the Turkish mines. But he was to be defeated by shortage of powder, of timber for shores and props, and of labour. Above all, labour. If the Turks did not have 'thousands of miners' as the chroniclers relate, they had far more than the defenders, and their men were trained for the task. Also, the counterminer was at the frequent disadvantage of starting after his adversary. It was a race, under-ground, calling for great physical endurance by relays of men working on their knees, in a space three feet by five feet at most, and in a foul atmosphere only made breathable at all by ventilation at intervals and, perhaps, by bellows and leather hoses. The miners were backed up by slaves and Rhodian volunteers with baskets for transporting the earth and rock out of the galleries, and followed by the carpenters – or shipwrights – with the props and shores. Above ground, the continuous reverberations of the cannon fire menaced the sweating miners with the danger of rock falls behind them.

Against most weapons, the individual Knight was still largely protected by his armour. In 1480 parade armour had not attained the fashionable eccentricity of the fluted, etched, gilded and enamelled 'Maximillian' splendours of the sixteenth century, and we may also forget about the elaborate jousting armour, with its exaggerated helm, as a mere status symbol – like hunting pink. Drawings and portraits of Grand Masters and Grand Crosses in full panoply are misleading. In 1770 – three centuries after Rhodes – the Grand Master Pinto is pictured (by Bernard) clothed in a suit of armour which would not have been unfashionable in 1480 and which he certainly never wore in anger. But the foot combat armour still to be seen in the palace of Valletta, used in 1565, is not very different from D'Aubusson's own fighting armour with its plain surfaces of modelled steel, close helmet and all-round cuisses to the legs, quilted arming cap and padded lining, the round, waist-length breastplate being reinforced in the lower part by an extra plate called a 'paunce' or 'plackart' curved to a point in front.[14] We know that he also had parade armour which he wore on ceremonial occasions.

Besides the more expensive custom-built armour affected by the senior officers, there was the munition armour, of a standard pattern, with interchangeable pieces, part of the general issue held by each Auberge and supplied to the rank and file of the Knights and Servants-at-Arms.

Full armour was probably not worn very frequently. Certainly, on shipboard, a simple skirted breastplate and open helmet were more practical. We read of the Grand Master being wounded in the thigh by an arrow, when on the battlements in 1480, and of his helmet being shot from his head – scarcely possible had it been of the close, laced-on pattern of full armour. In 1522 eye injuries and leg wounds were frequent.

The common foot-soldier did not wear armour; but he was tolerably well protected – and more mobile – in his 'jack', a canvas jacket reinforced internally with plates of metal or horn, topped by a 'kettle hat' or 'sallet', or a Spanish 'cabacete' – all very similar to the various 'tin hats' of modern armies.

Armour would resist crossbow quarrels and spent or glancing bullets; but the fully armoured knight came into his own in the hand-to-hand fighting in the breaches where he stood like a one-man tank, swinging his great sword or jabbing and thrusting with short pike or 'partisan' (the point of the sword was seldom used, crushing, severing strokes at the neck and limbs being preferred), while the bowmen and the arquebusiers fired over his shoulders or kept up a cross-fire into the press of the advancing infidels.

The Ottoman land forces were the most highly organized army in the world. Around a regular, standing army composed of the Janissaries – originally a body of praetorian infantrymen, but later to become a self-contained army embodying every specialization – and the feudal militia, who were land-holders liable for military service whenever called upon, there were grouped the Sipahis, who were gunners, armourers, smiths and marines, normally hired for a single campaign, and the Piyade, land-holding infantrymen, with the irregular Azab and Bashi-Bazouk, who were mercenaries serving for loot and plunder. A light cavalry force, the Akibi, were also mercenaries bent on loot.

The Janissaries were the *corps d'élite*. Taken from Christian parents at the age of ten to twelve as part of the recognized tribute due to the Sultan, they were educated in the strictest orthodoxy of Islam, celibate and trained in all the military skills. The Janissaries had a great deal in common with the Knights of the Hospital, by whom they were regarded as worthy opponents.

The feudal militia had a built-in command structure related to the individual's stake in the empire. The smallest hereditary fief was the Timar, larger and more valuable was the Ziamet – involving greater obligation to furnish men and equipment. The largest of the Ziams became Pashas, Beys, Sanjakbeys and Beylerbeys, with appropriate command and administrative responsibilities in the army and civil government.[15]

Each unit in the Ottoman forces wore a distinctive uniform, which had obvious advantages in battle, and if the Christians were not frightened by the trappings of the Janissaries they were certainly impressed by them. The Knight Sir Nicholas Roberts, writing in 1523 to his uncle the Earl of Surrey after the fall of Rhodes, says: 'They wear on their heddes a long white cape [?cap] and on the top of the cape a white ostrage which gevith a great show. . . .'[16]

The Ottomans never favoured plate armour, preferring the lighter mail, with riveted or solid links, and a spiked open helmet, usually of turban shape, with sliding nose-piece. The Anatolian Turks wore both mail and breastplates. The Ottoman equivalent of parade armour included fluted helmets, damascened in gold, brigandines (a kind of armoured jacket) with exposed gold rivets, and heavy cloaks with luxuriant decoration. Since the scimitar was a weapon without defensive value, they also continued to use the small, circular shield, or target, after it had gone out of fashion in Europe. In close, hand-to-hand work the Turkish armour was much less efficient than that of the Christians, who were able to risk their persons with greater boldness.

It was the Ottoman practice to send in the Bashi-Bazouk first. A rascally crew, many of whom were Christians – Slavs, Hungarians and Germans – fighting for plunder, they were excellent in the first shock of an assault, but easily discouraged if they were not immediately successful and the hopes of plunder receded. A line of military police armed with whips and maces therefore advanced behind them, ready to chastise the waverers. Behind the police came the Janissaries waiting to cut down any fugitive who got that far. The lot of the Turkish cannon-fodder was not happy. Against well-armed, disciplined defenders they were often handicapped by their own numbers and got in each other's way. A single cannonball, or a great rock from a trebuchet, would kill several at a time, and in scaling assaults most of the attackers could expect to be cut down before they reached the top of the ladder. But the irregulars wearied the defenders, and their corpses filled the ditches, so that by the time the Janissaries were thrown in the defence had weakened, and there would usually be no thought of retreat.

The Ottoman military machine suffered from three great defects. Its monolithic structure made the empire particularly vulnerable to a war on two fronts: pressure in the west was immediately relieved by any warlike attitude on the part of the Persians. And remarkably few, not only of the Ottoman generals but of the common soldiers, were Turks. Many were not even Muslim. Above all, it was inflexible and over-centralized. The Sultan's absolute, supreme command cramped initiative in his generals, who were all too often the hapless victims of moments of imperial rage: fear of public disgrace, the bastinado and the stake are not always the best inducements for a soldier.

As the range and weight of artillery grew, the Holy Religion was compelled to spend more and more of its energies and its resources on modernizing the defences of Rhodes, of St. Peter and of the island outposts.

The first need was for thicker walls and gun-ports; but the walls were soon too thick for the defenders to watch the ground immediately below them, and the first gun-ports were without the external splay which allowed guns to be effectively trained.

Breaches made by cannon-fire rendered the old high, unscalable curtain defences, the machicolations and the hourds virtually useless. The need for flanking fire gave rise to the bastion – a solid construction projecting from the curtain and of about the same height, and presenting an angle to the field whence cannon (as well as bows and smaller fire-arms) could cover any assault on the curtain, and any blind spots from the neighbouring bastion.[17]

At first compromises were made. Many of the thirteen towers were cut down and strengthened with earthen parapets of low 'command' – fifteen to thirty feet – and ditches were deepened and widened, giving a height of forty to sixty feet from the bottom of the ditch to the top of the earthwork. The escarp (or wall of the ditch nearest the defence) and counterscarp, nearest the enemy, were revetted with masonry. Subterranean chambers were excavated in the bottom of the ditch to provide direct fire along the bottom. But it was not until 1496 that the first true bastion was built (from a design by Francesco di Giorgio) at the post of Auvergne.

With the development of step-by-step defences, Rhodes by 1522 had one of the most modern systems anywhere: from ditch to ravelin (built in front of the curtain to resolve the difficulty presented by the fact that the salient angles of the bastion supplied a safe assembly point for the attackers), thence to rampart, bastion and tower. The enemy must pound away with his cannon for days, perhaps weeks, before there was a sufficient breach to justify a mass attack. And, even then, there was the murderous cross-fire, and the retrenchments – ditches and earthworks erected by the defenders in way of the breach – to be met. Positions were then temporarily reversed, and a determined defender might continue for a very long time, fighting from retrenchment to retrenchment, and sometimes beating the attacker back beyond his point of entry.

The attacker required a clear foreground for his guns, but with sufficient cover for his infantry and arquebusiers. Invariably he dug in. Trenches were ideally deep enough to enable a standing man to fire his weapon – say six feet, and eight to ten feet wide, with an earth-covered timber roof. The sides were revetted with gabions – cylinders made of flexible branches filled with earth and small stones. Gabions were used, too, to erect palisades around the siege batteries and the approaches were protected against sorties with *abbatis* of pointed tree trunks, pegged to the ground.

But the entrenchments were not static. Day after day they would creep, like so many snakes, nearer to the counterscarp of the ditch, and then under and beyond it until enemy miners could be heard working under the very foundations of the city.

The navy of the Order, which rarely exceeded five galleys and a carrack or 'great ship', with a number of smaller craft in full commission,[18] supplemented whenever necessary by privateers and corsairs chartered or operating under the Grand Master's licence, played little offensive part in either of the two sieges. The carrack, as its name implies (from the Italian *caricare*: to load), was primarily a cargo and troop transport. Usually of some 500 to 700 tons burden, the 'great carrack' could be up to 2,000 tons, and the Knights actually built one (the *St. Anne*) of 4,000 tons. These 'great' ships were the largest in the world, with three or four decks up to eight feet high, and with poop and prow overtopping the main deck by twenty feet. No unspliced tree was large enough for a mainmast. The whole company of 200 men and two heavy capstans were needed to hoist the main yard, and in bad or squally weather it had to be lowered and hoisted several times a day. Good sailers with a soldier's wind astern, they were the unhandiest ships afloat with a wind on the bow. Within limits, even the smallest carrack could mount heavier armament than the galleys; but until the introduction of the lower deck gun-port (in 1515 in England and in 1523 in the Order's carrack *St. Anne*) they were no match for them. Essentially, they were not warships.

Once a full-scale invasion was on foot the Order could not risk an offensive role at sea, because there were not enough men to man the fleet and to defend Rhodes. A gallant dash at the Turkish armada would probably not have destroyed enough of the enemy (there were at least fifty vessels in 1480 and more in 1522) to send them home, and it would certainly have cost too many Knights and skilled soldiers for the safety of the Convent. The greater part of the crews and fighting complement were disembarked; but a number of vessels were able to keep the sea and to maintain communications with the outposts, with Crete and Cyprus and with Europe. Many of these, it seems, were brigantines – ships up to 250 tons burden, though it is difficult to be certain of their size, because tonnage references in the fourteenth and fifteenth centuries are rough estimates of capacity. 'Tons burden', 'tuns' and 'tunnage' all differ.

A brigantine is strictly a two-masted vessel with a square-rigged foremast and a boom-sail on the mainmast. The term was used loosely to cover any kind of small ship, i.e. not a galley, and not a specialized fighting craft. There were also small galleys with single rowers on each side forward of a single mast, and pairs aft, ideal for inter-island and coasting work.

The Ottoman blockade was never effective, and some supplies and reinforcements were able to get in from Europe and from Crete. But, short of a large European relief force, the Order's maritime resources were inadequate to maintain reinforcements and fresh supplies of victuals and munitions indefinitely.

The Ottoman fleets included two-masted triremes, lateen-sailed, with rowing benches all on one level seating three rowers, each with a single oar on a separate thole-pin, but all three projecting through one port; slightly smaller biremes, or *fustae*; large galleys and *parandarie*, heaving sailing barges for transporting cannon and stores; brigantines, sloops, cutters and several 'great ships'. The Turks relied heavily on renegade Greeks, Venetians and Genoese for their sea-power, for they were not, themselves, natural seamen.

Christian and Turk alike were alive to the value of sound as a weapon of morale. Cannon were sometimes fired for no other reason than their frightening noise. The Christians had a wide choice of musical instruments, but they seem to have been content with trumpets, kettledrums and fifes for martial purposes. For general alarms and for celebrations they used the church bells. If they ever went into action at Rhodes with a band, no contemporary notices the fact. We are only told about a defiant flourish of trumpets and the drums beating to quarters. The Turks, on the other hand, rarely advanced without a martial din of ear-splitting and terrifying volume, which the chroniclers duly note. The bands of the Janissaries, both foot and mounted, put heart into the lesser breeds of the mercenary troops, and accompanied the warlike songs which cheered them on their long, plodding marches across Asia. The music was unearthly and

barbaric to the Christians, who wrote of the devilish screams and
the clashing of cymbals which almost invariably preceded an
attack as if they thought that they were no more than part of some
uncoordinated, primitive war dance.

The Janissaries used oboes, of a particularly shrill tone,
triangles, jingling crescents and cymbals, as well as trumpets and
kettledrums. And it was to the sound of these – so loud, say the
chroniclers, that it drowned the sound of the guns – that they
advanced through a hail of fire, in close order, keeping perfect
dressing, closing their ranks as soon as a man fell.

The Turkish custom of heralding their attacks with songs and
music deprived them of the advantage of surprise. They were not
inhibited from night fighting by any fancy idea that it was
ungentlemanly, like the Christians before the French Wars in
Italy; but we may suppose that in a superstitious age the darkness
held terrors of its own. For the many Christian renegades in the
Turkish lines there were the wandering, restless souls released for
an hour or two from Purgatory, for whose repose they ought to
have been praying. For the Muslim, too, there were fearsome
spirits of darkness. This may explain why, even as a prelude to a
night attack, the Turks often bartered surprise for the comforting
crash of cymbals and the high screech of the oboe, loud enough
to scare off any spirit, Christian or Muslim; while some ulema
led them in chants uncomplimentary to the enemy, announcing
the certainty of rich loot and fair Rhodian maidens.

As to the size of the forces engaged, the numbers of ships used
and, very particularly, the casualty reports for both sieges, great
caution is necessary. We have only to recall the published figures
during the Battle of Britain in 1940 to appreciate that propaganda
statistics are not peculiar to the fourteenth and fifteenth centuries.
It is a matter of degree. The Christians, reporting the actions at
Rhodes, overstated enemy numbers and enemy casualties and
understated those of the defenders.

Even recent estimates of the Turkish forces (e.g. those of Rossi)
are unreliable. Statements about the strength of the fleet in 1480
vary between 100 and 160 vessels. The lower figure is still too
high, and we should remember that victuals ('on the hoof'),
ammunition, support troops and necessary camp followers could

be ferried from Marmarice as convenient. The Spanish Armada, intended to support and protect a convoy with an army large enough for a serious invasion of England, consisted of sixty-five 'great ships', twenty-five stores ships, four galleases and four galleys, manned by some 31,000 people.

Some idea of the complement of the largest carrack may be had from the Order's gigantic 4,000 ton *St. Anne*, of 1523. She was designed for a fighting complement of '300 besides 400 infantry and cavalry'. There were no comparable 'great ships' in the Turkish fleet in 1480 or in 1522.

In 1480, the garrison in Rhodes may have numbered 2,000 of all arms. For the invading force a total of 15,000 (not all of whom would be actively engaged at one time) is more likely than the spurious defector Master George's incredible figure of 100,000.

For 1522, Bosio gives a Turkish figure of 200,000 troops, of whom 50,000 were miners. Rossi, relying on Turkish sources, details 40,000 sailors and galley slaves, 20,000 Azab (irregulars), 10,000 Janissaries, 100,000 mixed troops from Rumelia and Anatolia, plus the reinforcements from Egypt and Syria which arrived during the siege.

As to the fleet, Turkish sources speak of 500 galleys, 100 'mahons' and 'bastards', and 100 small craft; and, elsewhere, of a total of 664 vessels. Sanudo gives 300 vessels: Bosio 130 galleys and 35 galleases, 15 mahons, 80 fustae, 'many brigantines' and ten or twelve 'great ships', with barges for heavy artillery.

All these figures are naturally suspect. Modern historians cannot accept that the Turks could ever have mustered, fed, armed, equipped and paid 200,000 men. Such an army was not really needed to besiege Rhodes – not the biggest of cities – and how could they have been usefully deployed? It has also been calculated that a fleet of 60 galleys, with supporting vessels, would give absolute mastery in either the eastern or the western Mediterranean. There is a poor case for an army of more than 20,000. The chronicler and eye-witness habit of borrowing Old Testament rhetoric, with its favourite figures of 60,000 and 100,000 and multiples of these, is firmly discredited by historians. As to the casualty figures, they too are ludicrously high. Such few official records as exist all deal with relatively modest numbers.

Pius II at Ancona in 1464, from a fresco
by Pinturicchio in the Cathedral, Siena

Mehmet the Conqueror, from a painting
attributed to Gentile Bellini

What we know of populations, logistics and food supply all points to the smaller figures and one should often divide the chroniclers' figures by ten. But reliable statistics simply do not exist.

Man for man and weapon for weapon, the Holy Religion was superior; but the Hospitallers were matched against the greatest military power in the world, and they were hampered by a web of intrigue, espionage and treachery both within and without their gates.

4

THE SIEGE
1480

There are no reliable contemporary portraits of Pierre D'Aubusson, the hero of 1480. The traditional medallions of the Grand Masters reproduced in editions of the *Statuta* of the Order, and converted into popular engravings for sale in Malta as late as the early years of the last century, show D'Aubusson, in 'choir dress', as a clean-shaven, round-faced, heavily built, ageing man with a fleshy nose, a small full-lipped mouth and wide-set, candid grey or blue eyes in which the engravers have faithfully repeated the unusual suspicion of a twinkle. A recent portrait by the Italian artist Renzo Basile, after a reconstruction by the Chevalier Mario Costarella,[1] is not a great deal more revealing. It portrays the Grand Master, in foot-combat armour, surcoat, Marshal's baton, and conventional, princely stance against a background of shattered battlements. The fleshy nose has been refined, there are the furrows of command on his brow and a hint of grey in the receding brown hair and neatly clipped beard (the Grand Master was fifty-seven in 1480), but there is no twinkle.

Every Grand Master – even self-confessed sybarites like De Paule and Pinto, or unpopular tyrants like Ximenes – has suffered from the gilt layers of canonization which the pious centuries have imposed, concealing from us his human vices and his human virtues. But His Eminent Highness Pierre D'Aubusson, Cardinal Prince of the Church, has suffered less than most. One of the more obvious candidates for canonization, he was nevertheless a figure whose legend was written, printed and widely read in his own lifetime, and some of his humanity has survived. We are told a little story of a sly joke at the expense of the ambitious young Chevalier Del Carretto when the Grand Master's helmet was shot from his head in the heat of battle. We hear of his tears at parting from his guest (and hostage), the young Turkish pretender Djem, and we can read his moving summons to the whole Order to come to the defence of the Convent. We can also read his factual, soldierly narrative of the siege, in which he makes light of the wounds from which he all but died.

The historian Pantaleone[2] says that D'Aubusson was 'of fine person and acute intelligence and easily captured the friendship of anyone who met him and whose affection he studied to win'.

D'Aubusson was born in 1423 on the family estate in La Marche, in the heart-land of France; second son of Renaud, Lord of Monteil and Viscount of La Marche, and the noble Lady Marguerite Chambon.[3] The D'Aubussons had been hereditary, semi-independent Seigneurs since the tenth century, ruling a territory bounded on the north by Berri and Bourbonnais, with Poitou to the west and Auvergne to the east. Their ancient capital was Guêret.

Born and bred at the centre of European chivalry, young Pierre could scarcely help being the very archetype of the Christian knight, with a fierce devotion to France (he was seven years old when St. Joan was burnt in the market place of Rouen), but above all to Christendom and to Holy Mother Church.

Porter[4] has a typical English Victorian comment. 'The ramifications of D'Aubusson's family,' he says, 'included in their limits a connection both with the Dukes of Normandy and also with the Saxon Kings of England; so that *although a Frenchman* by birth and education there must ever exist a sympathy for his high name and gallant achievements on this side of the channel.'

To the usual upbringing of a son of a noble house, young Pierre had added the wider education of the dawning Renaissance under the wing of the Emperor Sigismund, and he seems to have been intended for a life at court. His first campaign was with the Dauphin (later Louis XI) against the Swiss in 1444. He also saw service with the new Royal Army of Charles VII, and doubtless learned something of the use of artillery. He was, however, not much over twenty-one when he journeyed to Rhodes, with letters of recommendation from his monarch, and was very readily accepted into the Langue of Auvergne. Almost before he had completed his novitiate he was awarded a Commandery.

In 1454 he was an obvious choice for the delicate task of touring Europe in the name of the Grand Master de Lastic, seeking aid against the awaited Turkish attack. Not unexpectedly, he obtained the handsome sum of 100,000 scudi (about £12,500) from Charles VII; but was otherwise unsuccessful in bringing back anything more than brittle promises.

Under de Lastic's successor, yet another fellow Auvergnat, de Milly, D'Aubusson fought in the defence of Kos in 1457, and in the abortive Cyprus campaign of 1459. It was he who advised the Aragonese Grand Master Zacosta (1461–7) to fortify the galley port by building Fort St. Nicholas (at the expense of the Duke Philip of Burgundy, Pope Pius II's only staunch ally).

Under the Italian Grand Master Orsini – whose election was a happy piece of papal nepotism – we find Pierre D'Aubusson elevated to the post of Captain General of Rhodes, spending every scudo he can extract from the rich Grand Master's private fortune on the modernization of the defences. A new curtain, 400 feet long and 20 feet high, was erected on the seaward approaches to the city, and the continuous ditch of the enceinte was everywhere deepened and widened.

In 1470 D'Aubusson commanded the Order's squadron which had been sent to help Venice hold Euboea against the Ottomans – an attempt rendered vain by the desertion of the Venetian fleet at the critical moment.

During the last three years of Orsini's reign, the old and frail Grand Master virtually abdicated his powers to D'Aubusson – now Prior of Auvergne – who pressed on with his preparations to receive the Turk. Three new towers were erected, and a boom defence consisting of a huge chain attached to baulks of timber was manufactured for the protection of the commercial harbour.

When Orsini died, D'Aubusson's election was a matter of form.

D'Aubusson's enemy, Mehmet II, was born at Adrianople on 30th March 1432, and, since he was to grow up to be the terror of the world, we know a good deal about him. We have Gentile Bellini's portrait in the National Gallery, painted in November 1480, when he was forty-eight: 'handsome, of middle height but strongly built. His face dominated by a pair of piercing eyes under arched eyebrows, and a thin, hooked nose that curved over a mouth with full red lips. In later life his features reminded men of a parrot about to eat ripe cherries.'[5]

His manner was dignified, rather distant, except when drunk,

which was too often for him to be accounted devout. He was
only gracious – even cordial – to scholars and artists. His upbringing and his station, perhaps more than his own nature, made him
secretive and distrustful. He had no desire for popularity; but his
intellect, drive and tenacity commanded respect.

Mehmet had had an unhappy childhood. Brought up at
Adrianople in exile from his father's court – for the Sultan
Murad preferred the sons of his noble wives – by his mother, a
Turkish slave-girl called Huma Hatun, and a formidable and pious
nurse called Daye Hatun, he was almost uneducated until, at the
age of eleven, he was summoned by his father to be trained for
the succession.

Some legend – and Mehmet himself encouraged the story – had
it that Huma Hatun was, in fact, a Frank. Certainly, the strain of
Othman's Asiatic blood was thin in him. His ancestors had
married and borne heirs by Greeks, Serbians and Albanians.
The turban apart, Bellini's portrait would serve for any renaissance European prince. Mehmet's father, Murad, was basically a
man of peace, and deeply religious. He had many Christian
friends – as well as a Christian, Serbian wife; but his essentially
defensive wars had left the Ottoman empire orderly and prosper-
ous. His eldest son Ahmet died suddenly at Amasia in 1437; and
the second son died in mysterious circumstances, suggesting
assassination, in the same city in 1443. Murad wished to retire to
a Dervish monastery and end his life in contemplation and prayer.
Shocked at Mehmet's lack of schooling, his father now subjected
the young man to an intensive course of science and philosophy,
Islamic and Greek literature, Turkish, Greek, Arabic, Latin,
Persian and Hebrew.

After his victory at Varna in 1444, Murad abdicated in favour
of Mehmet – now twelve – leaving the young Sultan under the
tutelage of his old and trusted Vezir Halil Pasha; but Mehmet's
arrogance and thirst for conquest would not suffer advice – he
wanted to attack Constantinople at once – and Murad had to
return. For a time he thought of disinheriting Mehmet in favour
of Ahmet, the infant son of one of his high-born wives, the
daughter of Ibrahim the Chandaroglu Emir; but when Murad
died, in February 1451, no one disputed Mehmet's succession
except the Prince Orkhan, eldest son of the Sultan Bajazet, a

hostage in Constantinople for whose safe keeping the Emperor received a handsome pension.

The way was now clear for Mehmet – or, perhaps, as he thought, not quite clear; for 'while he was giving a gracious welcome to his father's widow, who came to offer her condolences on Murad's death and her congratulations on Mehmet's succession . . . his servants hastened to the harem to smother her young son Ahmet in his bath'.

It was said that the new Sultan had set himself two great tasks – the conquest of Constantinople and the destruction of the Holy Religion in Rhodes. But the dominant Turkish motive in the fifteenth century was probably sheer greed for land, revenue and slaves; while Mehmet the Conqueror's own personal craze was for acquiring cities famous in classical antiquity, such as Constantinople, Rhodes and Athens. His biographers say that he wanted to be a second Alexander the Great.

Intellectual, wine-bibber, murderer, homosexual; a tyrant hailed as 'the Padishah, whose army is the host of Angels. The Protected of Allah, whose companion is Khidr,[6] assisted by the favour of God and divine inspiration'; yet Mehmet II was devoted to the memory of his mother, and was capable of chivalry, kindness and tolerance.

Mehmet was strangely reluctant to attack Rhodes. His preoccupations with the eastern Europeans, the Venetians, the Egyptians and the Persians do not entirely account for his reluctance. It seems that he would seriously have welcomed an accommodation with the Holy Religion, and his envoys made repeated overtures to the Grand Master. If Demetrios Sophianos (a renegade Greek from Euboea, who was sent as ambassador to Rhodes in 1476), was to be believed, the Sultan would have been satisfied with a purely nominal tribute and an agreement to leave his seaborne trade unmolested. Indeed, Mehmet went so far as to interpret some trifling gifts brought to him by an envoy of D'Aubusson as tribute, and the envoy was under the embarrassing necessity of publicly contradicting him.

D'Aubusson for his part did not trust the Turks, and even less their Greek envoys. In the matter of tribute he temporized, saying that he must refer the question to his religious superior, the

Holy Father in Rome. The breathing space enabled him to re-inforce his outposts at St. Peter and the outlying islands, to lay in stocks of grain and powder and shot, and to gather such reinforce-ments as he could from Europe. Still Mehmet hesitated.

Another renegade, a Rhodian of good family called Antonio Meligalo, who had 'squandered his patrimony in debauchery',[7] accompanied Sophianos to Constantinople on his return, carrying with him some out-of-date plans of the city and fortifications, and a number of inaccurate reports about the Order's state of preparedness. It does not seem to have occurred to Caoursin, or to any other contemporary, that Meligalo may have been a double agent – there were plenty of them about. Meligalo said that Rhodes was ripe for conquest. The citizens were disaffected. The Knights, particularly the Italians and the Spaniards, were near mutinous. The towers and the curtains of the post of Auvergne were old and dilapidated (which was true – the fine, new bastions and lower, thick walls of the 'Boulevard' of Auvergne were not completed until 1496). The city, he said, was virtually wide open.

In Constantinople, Sophianos and Meligalo had found an ally in a traitor of quite different calibre. He was George Frapan – variously described as Frapanus, Frapan, and Frapant, Frepant and Frepand, or simply as 'Master George' – a German military engineer and artillery expert who was held in the highest esteem by Sultans and Vezirs alike. Together, the plotters approached Misac Palaeologos Pasha, said to be a renegade prince of the house of Palaeologos. If Misac (or Mesih) was indeed a Palaeolo-gos, his connection with the imperial line must have been fairly remote, and he can hardly have been in the direct line of either of the two imperial houses;[8] but the authorities agree in describing him as 'a Greek Pasha of the noble Palaeologos family',[9] and as 'a renegade, a Greek of the Imperial house of Palaeologos, who, at the capture of Constantinople had forsworn his religion, and taken service under Mehmet . . . ever ready to persecute his former faith . . . amongst whom the Knights of Rhodes had been distinguished by his bitterest animosity.'[10]

The little cabal now spent three years lobbying the Vezirs and pressing the Sultan to mobilize a fleet and an army for the descent on Rhodes, with Misac as Vezir and Commander-in-Chief.

At length, in the winter of 1479, the campaign opened with a costly reconnaissance in force led by Misac. His galleys landed cavalry and Sipahis at remote points in Rhodes, who struck inland, ravaging the countryside and burning villages.

D'Aubusson's spies had given warning of the approach of Misac, and the people had taken shelter in the castles. There was little booty to be had, and when the landing parties began to reassemble they found their retreat barred by armoured men. The survivors who reached the beaches scrambled incontinent into their boats, and Misac made hasty sail for the neighbouring island of Tilos where he hoped for an easier prey. But the garrison here had been reinforced, and the Turks were once more chased away with heavy losses.

Misac's raiding squadron spent the rest of the winter at Physcos (Marmarice), eighteen miles across the strait from Rhodes, and an ideal assembly port for such an expedition as he purposed.

Physcos (now called Marmaris Limani) is protected from the south by the peninsula of Nimaria Adasi, the southern extremity of which is Red Cliff Point. The harbour is land-locked and affords a secure anchorage with good holding ground in depths from seven to twenty fathoms. The north-west shore is bounded by a plain with several small streams running through it. The hills are covered with pine trees, and the country is very fertile. The distance overland from the Hellespont is something over 200 miles.

Meanwhile, an army said to number 70,000, with horses, mules, cannon, munitions and all the impedimenta of a siege train, was assembled at Constantinople. The troops were to march and ride overland from the Hellespont to Physcos. The heavy stores and the siege cannon were to go by sea, and the whole force would rendezvous at Physcos.

It was April 1480 before the army had assembled, and D'Aubusson was now kept informed almost hour by hour of the Turkish activities. Some attempt was made to conceal the preparations. Mehmet closed all his ports to foreign shipping, and double agents were sent to Rhodes with false stories, such as that Mehmet was dead, or that the fleet was destined for Alexandria.

But D'Aubusson pressed on with his arrangements. The Rhodians were directed to gather their animals and their personal property, and to retire into the city and the fortified points, scorching the fields as they withdrew – but harvesting even the unripe crops that might serve as rations. The great chain of the commercial port was rigged, and those galleys and lighter craft which had not been dispersed to strategic ports were withdrawn behind it.

The defenders of Rhodes probably numbered no more than 600 Knights and Servants-at-Arms who were members of the Order, and perhaps as many as 1,500 mercenaries and local militia. Some reinforcements did reach them during the siege, and a notable addition to their power arrived shortly before the Turkish landing in the person of D'Aubusson's nephew Antoine, Count of Monteil, who was returning, with a considerable retinue, from a particularly opportune pilgrimage to the Holy Places. With him were six other Auvergnats with their train of professional soldiers. D'Aubusson had been granted plenary powers by the Council, and although Antoine was not a member of the Order (being married), he was appointed Captain General of the city.

The defenders were not at all dismayed. They had two years provisions and (as far as they could estimate) ample powder and shot for the same period. The cheerful and rather bloodthirsty Augustinian monk Father de Curti wrote to his brother in Venice that 'the City is well provided with grain, wine, oil, cheese, salted meat and other foodstuffs . . . many crossbows and both heavy and light guns and earthenware fire-pots and receptacles for boiling oil and Greek fire and pots full of pitch lashed together . . . and there is a continuous watch by day and night of select companies of crossbowmen and hand-gunners and 100 cavalry'.

The pleasant villas and the gardens in the approaches to the city had been levelled to provide as little cover as possible; but there were still too many walls and orchards.

Soon after dawn on 23rd May,[11] the look-out at the signal station on Mount St. Stephen sighted the Turkish armada, fifty or more sail strong, on a south-easterly course towards Akra Milos. They were a splendid sight: in rough crescent formation, with the slow, heavy transports in the centre and rear, and the triremes on either wing ready to repel any desperate attack by the galleys of the Order. 'The sea,' wrote de Curti, 'was covered with sails as far as the eye could see.' The sails shone like the wings of birds in the morning sun: the striped lateen sails of the galleys and the fustae, and the square sails of the carracks and the brigantines; and everywhere the white crescent of the Ottoman flashed on its blood-red ground and the horse-tail banners of the commanders of the Janissaries and the Sipahis fluttered in the wind.

In the city the drums beat to action stations, and the church bells pealed to warn the people and to call them to prayer. The miraculous ikon of Our Lady of Phileremos, which had been brought into the city from the monastery of Koskino, was exposed continually to the veneration of Latin and Greek alike.

But there were to be some hours of respite yet. The armada altered course off Akra Milos and made towards Marmarice, where the main landing force was now gathered after its long march overland. Misac Pasha, with Master George, was waiting there. The miserable Meligalo had died 'of a foul disease', and his corpse had been cast overboard on passage from Constantinople. Demetrios Sophianos, who had been joined by yet another renegade Greek, one Alexis of Tarsus, was with the fleet.

At dusk[12] – there is scarcely any twilight in these waters – the first of the transports and landing-craft (*parandarie*) began to arrive from Marmarice. They rounded Akra Milos and anchored in the Bay of Trianda where there is a good beach, sheltered and hidden by Mount St. Stephen from the east, and with several streams of fresh water even in summer. No serious attempt was made to resist the landing: D'Aubusson could not afford the manpower. Nevertheless, there were some hot-headed sorties, and the Turkish skirmishing parties, 'running about', says de Curti, 'like grunting swine rooting in a new pasture', suffered some casualties before night fell.

By dawn on 24th May the Turks had established their bridge-head and had advanced around the foot of Mount St. Stephen overlooking the city. Misac, the Commander-in-Chief, set up his pavilion on the slopes of the hill, and at once commenced to surround the city and to site a heavy siege battery, protected by gabions and abbatis, in the garden of the Church of St. Anthony on the mainland immediately opposite the Tower of St. Nicholas. D'Aubusson[13] says that this battery consisted of 'three great bronze basilisks of an incredible size and power, capable of firing balls of nine palms (about seven feet) in circumference'.

The Knights countered by mounting three bombards in the garden of the palace of Auvergne on the right flank of the Turkish battery, with which they could harass the guns' crews. There were more skirmishes outside the walls, and an Auvergnat Knight, the Chevalier Murat de la Tour, was killed; the first Christian casualty.

Before opening his bombardment of the city, Misac sent his herald to the walls calling upon the garrison and the citizens to surrender, and promising a general amnesty and special privileges to the Greeks. D'Aubusson disdained to reply, leaving it to the men-at-arms on the battlements to tell the herald in soldier's language to go away if he valued his head.

Misac's gunners now opened fire from every side, firing into the city with the hope of undermining the morale of the Greek citizens; but the great seventeen-foot basilisks opposite St. Nicholas were used at once in an attempt to destroy the stout tower which commanded the entrance to the galley port and which, in company with the batteries at the post of France, made an attack from seaward or landward upon the northern section of the city – which was also the Knights' quarter – virtually impossible. Once destroy St. Nicholas and occupy the mole, and the Turks could bring their ships into the port, prevent outside aid from reaching the city, and, perhaps, effect an entry by one of the two northern gates of St. Peter or St. Paul, thus outflanking the post of France.

Master George had boasted that 'no wall yet built could resist the fire of his artillery', and the first results of the general bombardment seemed to bear him out. D'Aubusson reported to the German Emperor Frederick III that within a few days the Turkish bombards had destroyed nine towers and razed the Grand Master's palace to the ground.

The cannonade certainly inspired terror amongst the townspeople. Father de Curti tells his brother that 'the ground trembled under his feet . . . no one from any nation had ever before seen such cannon . . . Had you been here, you would certainly have

*Rhodes encircled by the Turkish Army,
from a woodcut of 1496*

taken refuge in a cave!' But D'Aubusson had organized shelters for the old and infirm and the children, and the casualties were few. Continuing their terror tactics the Turks resorted to fireballs and incendiary arrows and bolts. D'Aubusson organized fire parties of men 'expert in the art', who extinguished every flaming projectile as it fell, 'and in this way much suffering was spared the Rhodians'.

The attack on St. Nicholas was less successful. Only after 300 rounds had been hurled at the twenty-four-foot thickness of the fort's ramparts did it begin to crack. The rate of fire was not very rapid – perhaps fourteen rounds a day for each basilisk, whose breech mechanism had to cool between rounds; and communication by way of the mole was never sufficiently interrupted by arquebus or crossbow fire from the opposite shore to prevent continuous supply and reinforcement of the tower. The Turks, too, were under constant cross-fire from the batteries in the city, and from the marksmen posted along the mole and in entrenchments which were constructed along the foreshore at the shallow, southern bight of the galley port, under the guns of France.

But once cracked, the huge stones of the westward rampart of St. Nicholas came tumbling down, bringing with them a great cloud of dust and mortar and opening the tower to the sky.

D'Aubusson knew that he must hold the ruins of St. Nicholas and the mole at all costs. The piles of cracked stone, and the loose aggregate which had held them in place, themselves offered first-class material for improvised defences. The ruin of St. Nicholas was soon as great an obstacle as ever. The mole, too, was converted into a continuous rampart. Hundreds of workpeople – slaves, soldiers, sailors, women – were occupied night and day excavating a trench along the summit of the mole, erecting timber palisades and shoring up the great heaps of rock and rubble around the base of the tower. A hand-picked company of Knights, under Fabrizio Del Carretto, was assigned to the defence of the tower, with supporting arquebusiers and archers. There were heavy losses on the mole; but Misac was not prepared for such tenacity. The destruction of the tower took longer than he had expected. The defenders continued their repair work and improvisations under fire; and by the time he could launch his main attack on the mole the improvised defences were nearly complete, and the shallow waters in the approaches to seaward had been filled with stakes driven into the sea bed.

At dawn on 28th May, a strange thing happened. In the half-light, the watch on the tower of St. Peter saw a tall, elegant figure standing on the far side of the ditch, waving and calling. A man-at-arms who had been a prisoner in Constantinople recognized the stranger as none other than the great Master George. He was asking to be let into the city. Interrogated by a German Knight, Master George protested that he had been moved by conscience as a Christian to desert his Muslim employers and to offer his services to the Holy Religion. D'Aubusson received him courteously and praised his decision, hoping that he would 'continue in his intention'. The deserter answered every question put to him about the strength and disposition of the enemy forces. There were, he said, about 100,000 men of all arms. The Turks had brought sixteen great ordnance, twenty-two palms (sixteen to seventeen feet) long, capable of hurling stone balls of nine to eleven palms (seven to nine feet) in circumference over a great range. Opinions about the sincerity of Master George's defection differed. Some were certain that it was a trick, and were for his immediate execution. This man, they said, 'whose work had been the ruin of so many Christian cities and the means whereby so many Christian virgins had ended their days in the Seraglio', was better dead, and that soon. Others were impressed by his suave and confiding manner, his eloquence and his charm – upon which latter point all were agreed; adding that certain other deserters, common soldiery of the Turkish irregulars, had it that Misac Pasha had fallen out with his expert, disappointed that the city had not fallen immediately to the power of Master George's artillery, and that the German dared not return to Constantinople.

D'Aubusson was not deceived; but he saw an opportunity of making use of the deserter's expertise. At the same time he appointed a robust and intelligent bodyguard of six Knights who were not to let the German out of their sight and were to report his every word and action.

Meanwhile, the bombardment of the city continued, still aimed primarily at the civil population, and the cannonade against St. Nicholas increased in fury as more heavy guns were moved to St. Anthony's garden. But on 1st June the Turks were unable to prevent a carrack from Sicily, with grain and reinforcements, from entering the commercial port. Neither were they able to prevent the departure of the Grand Master's dispatch vessel for Europe, bearing copies of his appeal, dated 28th May,[14] addressed to every member of the Order:

Brother Pierre D'Aubusson. . . . We, from the Convent . . . to each and every Prior, Professed Knight and Brother of our Order, in whatever place established . . . Greetings in the Name of Him who is the Salvation of us all. . . . That which the Emperor of the Turks has long designed against Rhodes he now purposes to achieve. That enemy of our Faith has long nourished for us and for our Order an implacable hatred because we resist him for the Faith of Christ. His rage mounts because, despite his conquest of Constantinople, twenty-seven years since, no part of our domain has fallen into his tyrannous power, and because we have defied his threats of force and have refused to pay the tribute demanded of us.

For these reasons he has lately made ready a powerful Armada of one hundred and nine vessels, enrolled soldiers from all the provinces near Rhodes, and has carried them from the mainland to our Island, invading our territory and, on 18th May [sic], set siege to our city. He has also brought a great many cannon, bombards and wooden towers with other engines of war, and has drawn up against us some 70,000 soldiers who assail us continually and press hard against us. . . . We resist with all our power and energy and with courage sustained by our Faith in the Mercy of God who never abandons them whose hope is in Him and who fight for the Catholic Faith. . . . We are no make-believe soldiers in fine clothes. Our men are no effeminate Asiatics. Their fidelity is proved and we have abundant cannon and bombards and good store of munitions and victuals. We will continue to confront the enemy while we await the aid of our Brethren. Above all we are sustained by our loyalty to the Holy Religion.

Moreover, the City of Rhodes – not without heavy cost – has walls, ramparts, moats and towers and we do not fear the enemy's power. Provided the help which our Brethren have promised arrives swiftly, the enemy will be constrained to abandon his enterprise and will be robbed of his design.

The tyrant flatters himself that he can wear us down with a long siege and diminish our forces, and tire our Knights, while he brings fresh soldiers from the mainland to replace the fallen. . . . But that furious great Dragon deceives himself. . . . By the help of Our Most Blessed Lord, our Knights and their Comrades-in-Arms will never desert this City of Rhodes, firm rock and foundation of our Order.

Neither does that enemy of our Faith understand that entry to our port is open and that it cannot be denied to anyone while the Westerlies blow in the Summer and Autumn, helping the prudent seaman who approaches by way of the Lician Sea. . . .

We have implored your help. In answering our pleas some have proved more obdurate and more idle than we could have believed possible. We have warned you. We have sought your aid. We have been answered with words. . . . You would not heed our warnings. Now believe the facts. . . .

Most Illustrious Brethren you see the danger by which we are beset. . . . Therefore, to the end that the Name of Christ be not shamed, We command and charge each and every one of you in the name of your Obedience; Venerable Priors, Bailiffs, Preceptors and Brethren of our Order to move with all haste to the succour of our City of Rhodes. . . . As well as winning the prize of Eternal Life you will earn fame and glory . . . or you will fall in the fight, which is a soldier's lot, and win the crown of martyrs. . . . What is more sacred than the defence of the Faith? What is happier than to fight for Christ? What is nobler than to redeem the promises which we made when we put on the habit of our Order? Not one of you may excuse himself. Not the aged or the infirm, not the poor . . . much less the young, the robust or the rich. . . .

D'Aubusson concludes his appeal on a practical note by granting a plenary faculty to mortgage all rents to the extent of three years value, in order to meet the charges and subsidies of the journey to Rhodes.

·   ·   ·   ·   ·

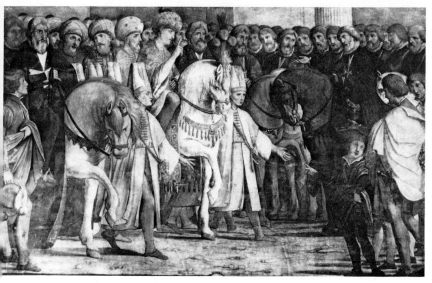

Misac Palaeologos Pasha before Rhodes in 1480

D'Aubusson welcomes the pretender Djem to Rhodes
in 1482, from frescoes by Mateo Perez de Alesio
in the Palace, Malta

Rhodes in 1486, from an engraving after Breydenbach

The first real trial of strength followed shortly upon the arrival of the grain ship. Misac was stung into action. One ship-load of grain and a hundred soldiers was not much; but without command of the port he could not stop such aid continuing indefinitely. And the Grand Master was trailing his coat. He had been rowed round the works on the mole and the Tower of St. Nicholas in his ceremonial gig, flying his personal standard; and he had been seen undeterred by the arquebusiers' shots falling around him, riding up and down the mole on a white Syrian charger, arrayed in his new parade armour with its gold damascene.

The first attempt on St. Nicholas came early in June after some ten days' continuous bombardment. The Turks embarked at Trianda in specially modified triremes from which masts and sails and all unnecessary rigging had been removed. Platforms had been built out over the bows, and the sides strengthened and protected with extra high bulwarks. Some mounted light cannon, and all were filled to the gunwales with Sipahis armed to the teeth. There was no attempt at surprise. Even before dawn the Turks set up a din – which they hoped was terrifying – of pipes and cymbals and drums and eldritch screams, as their men boarded the landing-craft and set off around the cape towards the galley port. The Knights were waiting for them with crossbow, longbow and arquebus, wild-fire pots and Greek fire. The guns in the ruins of the tower could not load fast enough to do much damage as the boats approached, and they were soon too near for the guns to be depressed so as to bear on them; but those which made for the inner end of the mole came under fire from the bombards on the walls of the post of France. The Sipahis – brave men with visions of Paradise before their eyes – plunged into the shallows or leapt from their platforms on to the as yet unfinished palisades. Some were tangled up with the stakes on the sea bottom and drowned where they fell. One of the triremes was set alight and blew up. Those of the Turks who reached the palisades were met by a wall of iron men, swinging their great swords, and a murderous cross-fire of bolts and arrows. They broke and fled back into the sea, throwing away their arms as they went.

As the remaining triremes drew rapidly off and away, the

wretched oarsmen being lashed into a frenzy of effort, they were pursued by bolts and arrows until they were out of range. It had been a foolhardy and ill-conceived attack. A trireme and at least half the attacking force had been lost. D'Aubusson dismisses it as 'an attack with moderately powerful forces . . . thinking success would be easy'. There were two more such attempts, which D'Aubusson passes over with the comment: 'Our people were on the alert and tenaciously maintained their posts until the beaten enemy retired.' There are no figures of casualties for any but the third of these attacks, said by de Curti to have been on 9th June (which was the feast of Corpus Christi). Both Caoursin and D'Aubusson say that deserters reported that the Turks lost 600 killed and as many wounded. We may take '600' to mean 'many'. There were apparently no casualties among the Knights. Losses among the common Christian soldiery were not reported unless the circumstances were unusual or bizarre.

It is possible that Misac, with characteristic Ottoman prodigality of lives in battle, intended no more by these earlier attacks than to test the strength of the defence. Already, by 7th June, he had shifted the main target of his heavy ordnance to the southern perimeter of the city in the sectors opposite the posts of England, Provence and Italy, which enclosed the Jews' Quarter. His plan was to attack simultaneously from north and south and thus divide the defence. Eight great basilisks concentrated on the tower and curtain of Italy, and one other was sited so as to range on the Tower of St. Angelo and the windmills on the eastern mole of the commercial port. At the same time, mortars hurled a continuous shower of shot and incendiaries into the thickly populated Jews' Quarter. The old fortifications here were a very different target from the new, robust tower of St. Nicholas. It soon became evident that they would not hold, and D'Aubusson set about ensuring that when the Ottomans poured through the breaches they would be met by a new line of retrenchments. He cleared the Jews' Quarter, demolishing every house and building. Every one available – men, women, children, priests, monks, nuns, freemen and slaves, knights and men-at-arms – was busy day and night erecting palisades, making gabions, digging trenches. Meanwhile the violence of Misac's bombardment never abated. The Franciscans were particularly energetic.

74

Pantaleone says that a popular Franciscan preacher, Fra Fadino, tucked up his habit, borrowed a mace, and plunged into the thick of the fight for the mole. D'Aubusson promised the Franciscans a new convent, and kept his promise. Caoursin had a word of praise for the Rhodians – and the Jews. 'Neither did the Grand Master, the Bailiffs, Priors, citizens, merchants, matrons, brides, maidens, spare themselves; but all carried on their backs stones, earth and lime; having no thought of personal gain but each thinking only of the safety of all.' Of the bombardment he says: 'The great projectiles from the mortars terrified the people who saw them flying through the air. . . . We ourselves were not a little anxious, particularly at night . . . which was spent in cellars, near the more robust doors or under the arches of Churches . . . snatching some restless sleep.' But so few people or beasts were killed by balls or falling masonry that all thought it a miracle. 'Among the inhabitants,' Caoursin goes on, 'who were from all nations, there was not one to be found who did not swear to never having seen or heard talk of such powerful engines of war.' Master George assured everyone – incautiously – that there were, indeed, no 'engines' like them anywhere in the world. Father de Curti, leading the people in prayer, admonishes the Almighty in truly Old Testament style:

Remember that You are called the
   God of Mercy and not the God of Vengeance.
Our sins, it is true, are more than the
   sands of the sea,
But remember Your Passion and Your
Bounty and hear our prayers,
To the end that the people shall not
say that Jesus is not their God!

Breaches were now appearing in the curtain of the post of Italy where the ditch gradually shallowed and ended, and was enclosed from the sea, thus offering an easier ascent to the enemy. The breaches were restored as they appeared, with stones and faggots and soil in which the balls buried themselves harmlessly.

The Turks had been busy, too, digging a complex of trenches,[15] snaking and zig-zagging towards the counterscarp of the ditch. At night, they brought up cart-loads of stone which they emptied into the ditch to fill it up to ground level. D'Aubusson's miners excavated a passage under the walls, and the Turks were dismayed to find their piles of stones diminishing as fast as they delivered them, as the miners drew them into their gallery and carried them back into the city.

Still the bombardment went on. D'Aubusson told the Emperor Frederick that 3,500 balls were launched against the walls in a space of thirty-eight days. It was not possible to remain on the walkways without taking cover, and a system of bells was arranged to warn sentries when they should come down by the ladders.

Meanwhile, Misac kept up his pressure on St. Nicholas. A great wooden tower, or 'belfry' was set up on the shore opposite the mole, and filled with archers and arquebusiers, protected by hides, who fired from their commanding platform at any movement. On 13th June a new and furious bombardment of the tower and mole commenced, and was kept up incessantly for four days and nights. Under cover of this barrage materials were brought overland from Trianda and a great pontoon bridge was constructed 'of planks connected with strong cross-pieces to which beams were fixed. The whole held together with nails', says Caoursin. The bridge was long enough to reach from the foreshore to the mole, and wide enough for six men to advance across it abreast. The idea was to float it into position by the aid of ground tackle, and a large grapnel had already been laid on the bottom near the tower, on the night of 17th June before moonrise, when an alert English sailor, one Roger Jervis,[16] caught the sound of muffled oars. Suspecting the enemy's purpose, but prudently waiting for the boat to make off in the darkness, paying out the hawser as it went, he dived in, sawed through the tackle with his poignard, and carried the grapnel triumphantly to D'Aubusson, to be rewarded with a present of a bag of gold.[17]

The night of 18th June was stormy. The Turks began soon after dark to manœuvre their pontoon into position, using rafts and oars. The Janissaries were assembled on the beach, and a strange fleet of modified triremes – thirty in all – with a dozen or more heavy store ships (*parandarie*) carrying cannon and powder and shot, and a flotilla of small craft, crept silently around Akra Milos.

The night attack on the Tower of St. Nicholas,
from a woodcut of 1496

The Janissaries marched on to the pontoon – six abreast and as steady as rocks. The pontoon was almost in position before the alarm was given.

Half the triremes had manœuvred close in to the seaward side of the tower and the remainder were approaching the inner side of the mole. Suddenly the cannon on the post of France and the terrace of the Grand Master's palace opened up, lighting the whole scene with their flashes. The leading ranks of the Janissaries were ashore, scrambling up the damaged glacis of St. Nicholas with ladders and hook-ropes. Fabrizio Del Carretto and his men had slept in their armour, and they fell upon the Janissaries with a will. Still they came on, while the Sipahis and the irregulars flung themselves at the defenders of the mole from both sides. But the pontoon could not survive. The guns of France had it at point blank range. A few more rounds, and the gunners found their target. The great pontoon, crowded with troops pressing forward to reach the tower, was crushed, and the Janissaries in their heavy, riveted brigandines and their flowing cloaks had to be strong swimmers indeed if they were to escape drowning.

D'Aubusson, who slept on the battlements, did not dare to reinforce the mole with troops from the Jews' Quarter – this was what Misac hoped – and Del Carretto was left to do his best. Nevertheless, D'Aubusson joined him, with his nephew Antoine, the Captain General, and together they performed prodigies. Antoine was evidently a large man. Seeing a Janissary nearing the top of the ramparts he 'picked up a heavy coffer and flung it at the man, splitting his skull'. It was during the night action that the Grand Master's helmet was struck from his head by a splinter of cannon-ball which had shattered on impact. At the Grand Master's side another splinter from the same ball killed a Rhodian called Agius.[18] Del Carretto begged the Grand Master to seek some less exposed position: 'The place of danger is my place,' replied D'Aubusson; 'if I should be killed, you will be able to worry about your own future, and not about mine.'

Fireships had been prepared and were now towed in amongst the Turks by some gallant Rhodian sailors. Four galleys and several *parandarie* laden with munitions were sent to the bottom. The fighting went on throughout the night. Wave after wave of attackers were flung back into the sea or slaughtered in the ruins of the tower and on the palisades of the mole. The carnage was lit up by gun-flashes, flaming arrows and bursting fire-pots, and a great pall of sulphurous smoke hung over the galley port.

By ten o'clock in the morning of 19th June, the Turks were exhausted. 'For three whole days,' wrote Caoursin, 'their corpses kept being washed up by the sea, glittering with gold and silver and rich raiment. Others could be seen on the bottom of the harbour, swaying with the currents as if put there by nature. . . . Not a few of our men collected the spoils, to their great profit.' Father De Curti reported that 'the heads of many Janissaries were displayed on our towers and the sea was red with their blood'.

One of the corpses washed up near the mole was that of Ibrahim Bey, a beloved son-in-law of the Sultan. Another was Merlah Bey, Admiral of the Galleys. Deserters reported the loss of 2,500 men by the Turks, certainly an exaggeration; but Misac Pasha was so overcome by the reverse that he retired to his pavilion and would see no one for three days. He may have been contemplating the fate of other unsuccessful Ottoman commanders.

The victory of St. Nicholas was celebrated with due pomp. The Grand Master rode through the city with the Grand Crosses and the Conventual Bailiffs all in their parade armour with the banners of the Order, the personal 'achievements' of the Commanders and the national Langues, and with bands of music and escorts of cavalry, afterwards going in procession for a solemn Te Deum in the Conventual Church.

But the expected stresses of a beleaguered city were beginning to show. Two mercenaries who had been caught throwing their arms into the sea, preparatory to deserting to the enemy, were publicly hanged. A party of Rhodian youths fighting amongst themselves in the streets were arrested and threatened with the gallows if they repeated the offence.

Some Italian Knights (of whom Merlo Piozzasco, the Admiral and Commander of the post of Italy, was certainly not one) had got wind of a dispatch from Constantinople announcing the imminent departure for Rhodes of the Sultan Mehmet himself with a fresh army of 100,000 men. The news was false; but they prevailed upon Gian Maria Filelfo,[19] D'Aubusson's Secretary, to approach the Grand Master with a suggestion that the Order abandon Rhodes before it was too late. D'Aubusson summoned the defeatists before him and informed them with a cold courtesy that 'since they were in such terror of Mehmet, they might leave the Convent at once, and he would personally cover their retreat; but if they remained there must be no more talk of surrender. If they continued their cabals, they knew what fate to expect'. Porter says that 'the Recusants threw themselves at his feet and implored him to give them an early opportunity of effacing the memory of their cowardice in the blood of the Infidel'.

Master George – still at liberty, though closely watched – was not the only distinguished deserter in the city. There were also one Gianni, said to be a Dalmatian, and an Epirote called Pizzio, both gentlemen of some substance who were acquainted with Maria Filelfo. The latter's innocent complicity with the Italian surrender 'plot' had put him in disfavour with D'Aubusson, and Pizzio was foolish enough to suppose that he could enlist his aid in a much more dangerous scheme – nothing less than the poisoning of the Grand Master. Filelfo led him on, until every detail of the plot had been exposed, and then reported to his master. Under 'the question', Pizzio confessed, and implicated Gianni. The Dalmatian was condemned to be beheaded, the Epirote to hanging. Neither of them reached the place of execution. The mob tore them in pieces on the way.

Arrows with messages attached were constantly being fired over the walls. Some warned the garrison against Master George. Others exhorted the native Rhodians in the name of the Pasha, their fellow Greek, to surrender, promising them the safety of their lives and property; and assuring them that the Sultan wished no ill to them, but only the possession of the city, the death of the Latin Knights and the destruction of their Order. If they decided against surrender, then Misac promised to exterminate them to the last soul. The attempts to subvert the loyalty of the Rhodians were vain. Misac now sent a herald to the Gate of Our Lady of Mercy, asking for a safe conduct. But D'Aubusson was letting in no more of Misac's men. He said that an envoy might come to the counterscarp and read aloud any message which the Pasha had for him. He would receive his answer from a spokesman on the

walls. The emissary – Suleiman Bey – duly arrived and declared
that the Pasha:

> ... marvelled not a little that you have resisted so far the power
> of a Sultan who has subdued two empires and so many king-
> doms, cities and provinces. If you care at all for your city and
> your country you will not let them suffer the cruel fate which
> further resistance will bring. The city will be devastated, the
> men slaughtered, the women ravished and consigned to
> ignominy. Reflect, therefore, whether war is better than peace.

Misac then offered favourable terms for a truce whereby the
Order might remain master of Rhodes – as vassal of the Sultan.

The spokesman of the Order was Fra Antoine Gualtier,
Castellan of the city. He was ready with his reply:

> We are unable not to marvel that the Pasha, with all his
> power and his great engines of war, should exhort us to peace –
> a word which ought to be foreign to those who stand in battle
> array. But he is much given to tempting souls with false words.
> Know then that neither your promises nor your offers of
> favours will move us to dishonour. Neither do your threats
> frighten us. We are one people, without difference as to Latin
> or Greek. We worship Christ with complete and utter convic-
> tion, and for Him we shall fight and meet death before we ally
> ourselves with Mahomet as your promises suggest. Take your
> armies home and send us ambassadors. Then we will talk of
> peace as equals; but as long as you stand armed before our
> city, do your duty as a soldier and, with the help of God, we
> will give you your answer. You do not have to do with effemi-
> nate Asiatics, but with Knights of proved valour. . . .

The reply may have been D'Aubusson's own composition.
He had a liking for the phrase 'effeminate Asiatic', which he also
uses in his summons to the Order.

The Turkish envoy retired, crestfallen, and the bombardment
re-opened with a new fury.

Master George, if indeed his part was that of a subtle Cassandra,
was not being subtle enough. He praised the defenders' courage
and the wisdom of the Grand Master's dispositions; but always
with a note of regret, as if to say: 'What a pity that such fine

fellows should be doomed!' He avoided overt alarm and despondency; but continually referred to the unprecedented power of the Turkish artillery. He was free with advice about the siting of guns. This was his undoing. It was noticed that shots from batteries re-sited by him always seemed to be followed by a redisposition of the enemy's batteries and a heavy bombardment aimed at the new sites, which – it was assumed – his expert eye had decided were weak. Summoned before the Council, his charm availed him nothing. He was put to the question and admitted, under the torture, that he was still Misac's man. His task had been to gain the confidence of the Grand Master, to undermine the morale of the defenders, and, at the right moment, to arrange a surrender. He was condemned and hanged, and a message announcing his fate was fired into the Pasha's camp. Confessions under torture are unsatisfactory; but no contemporary had any doubts about Master George's guilt.

The 24th June, Feast of the Patron St. John the Baptist, was celebrated with more than ordinary solemnity. The battered buildings and the churches which were still standing were illuminated, the bells were rung, and the Order assembled for High Mass in the Conventual Church. The besiegers were taken aback by this behaviour and thought that a relief force must have been sighted: they had themselves been cheered by the appearance of two great galleys from Syria with fresh companies of Janissaries. Very soon, indeed, some succour did arrive from Europe in the shape of a carrack, the *Palomari*, chartered and commanded by Benedetto della Scala, of the great family who played so large a part in the history of Verona, with a force of Veronese pikemen and arquebusiers. D'Aubusson had been right. The Turks were quite unable to prevent 'prudent seamen navigating by way of the Lician Sea' from entering Rhodes; but it was only a single ship.

Misac's batteries were creeping closer to the Jews' Quarter. Protected by gabions and abbatis, the culverins and mortars were now firing almost from the counterscarp itself. The curtain of the post of Italy was little more than a pile of rocks and rubble, sloping upwards from the half-filled ditch and inviting an attack. The tower of Italy stood – but precariously. A body of Italians – the same Knights who had felt the sharp edge of the Grand

Master's tongue – making their sortie into the bottom of the ditch, by way of the miners' tunnel on a moonless night, ascended the counterscarp and rushed the new batteries, setting fire to the timber defences and spiking the guns. The heads of the hapless Turkish gunners were brought back in triumph on the pikes of the Italians. D'Aubusson forgave them.

By the third week in July work was complete on the retrenchments facing the great breach in the curtain of the post of Italy. There was a deep, semicircular ditch, and, behind it, an earthwork constructed of soil, sand, rubble, branches and, finally, a wall two feet thick. The soil and sand had been wetted and had set like cement. The retrenchment commanded the approach from the breach, and the level ground between it and the ruins of the curtain had been 'booby-trapped' with ditches covered with light twigs and a layer of soil. Ample store of anti-personnel devices – Greek fire, casks full of pitch and sulphur, small *carcasses* full of iron fragments, and incendiary hoops designed to break the enemy's ranks – had been provided. But the weapon which chiefly delighted the Knights was an old-fashioned trebuchet which they christened 'The Tribute' (*tributo* for *tribuco*). The weapon had been unfashionable for so long that only a Basque sailor called Juan Aniboa knew how to construct it. Once built, it was simple enough to operate, and it wrought havoc with the Turkish trenches and batteries, hurling great masses of stone on to them, crushing men and wrecking the field works at every shot. Most important, it used neither powder nor shot and needed little skill.

The bombardment of the Jews' Quarter had now lasted five weeks. The ceaseless monotony, the clouds of black smoke, the deafening roar of the cannon, and the whistling of the flying stone as the balls broke into a thousand pieces on hitting the walls and the masonry, were beginning to shake the nerves of everyone from Knight to Jewish shopkeeper. When, therefore, at dawn on 27th July, the Turks began chanting battle songs and sounding their pipes and cymbals, and beating their drums, the defenders looked forward with something like relief to the impending battle. The din went on until dusk. The Knights replied with defiant fanfares on their trumpets, beat to quarters on their drums, and rang the bells. The walls flanking the breach and the retrenchments were manned with picked troops commanded by the most valiant Knights of every Langue; but under cover of nightfall, Misac brought up every basilisk, culverin, mortar and perrier in his armament, and the barrage which he now put up was so fierce that the walls could not be manned

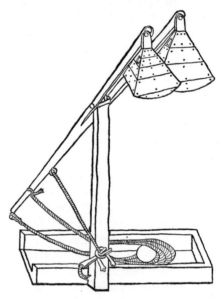

A trebuchet, loaded, before release

and the defenders were compelled to take cover behind the retrenchments. A final shower of threatening messages was fired into the city announcing that Misac had hoisted the black flag, which meant that the city would be sacked and its citizens slain or sold into slavery. The Knights would be impaled upon stakes,[20] and Rhodes would pass to the Sultan. The Muslim then performed their ablutions, turned towards Mecca and invoked God and his Prophet. At sunrise the bombardment ceased. There was a pause. Then a single gun signalled the advance.

A great wave of Bashi Bazouk irregulars rushed across the ditch and up over the piles of rubble where the wall had been. Armed with hook-ropes and javelins and pikes and torches to set fire to stockades, they scaled the ruins of the tower of Italy, from which the defenders had retired to shelter from the barrage; and there came that dreadful moment when the Rhodians saw the Ottoman standard flying from the tower.

After the Bashi Bazouks – the shock troops who fought in the hope of plunder – came the Janissaries, advancing at the double, keeping their ranks in perfect order, unbroken by the rain of missiles, arrows and javelins, stones and bullets which now descended on them from the post of Provence on their left flank.

The Turkish attack was not merely a headlong rush at the breach, and the scaling of the ruined wall near the tower of Italy was not an impulse. Nothing is more likely than that Misac had been fully informed of the progress of the retrenchment in the Jews' Quarter – agile and silent scouts could easily have crept up to the crest of the rubble 'hogsback' which led to the breach, and observed the progress of the defenders by moonlight.

The ditch and the wall, with its earthwork behind, completely enclosed a crescent-shaped area which had been cleared of buildings previously along with the rest of the Jews' Quarter. If the Turks could be tempted into this trap they were exposed to fire from behind the retrenchment as well as to cross-fire from the battlements of Italy and Provence on either flank. But there was a weakness at the horns of the crescent. Here the tattered and jagged ruins of the twenty-foot wall overtopped the wall of the retrenchment, and it was not a difficult ascent for a determined man. Beyond the tower of Italy a short length of wall with a single angle stretched towards the sea and the commercial port. The way into the city lay open for every Turk who could be got on to the walk-way in this area, and covering fire could be given from the tower itself.

D'Aubusson must have seen with horror the Turkish standard flying from the tower. He understood the danger at once. Already lame from an unhealed arrow wound in his thigh – and no longer young – he ran up the nearest ladder on to the walk-way, shouting orders as he went to smash all but the three ladders close to the breach which gave access to the Jews' Quarter. He was followed by a dozen or more Knights and by three standard bearers, and together they blocked the way, facing north and south, flailing about them with sword and mace. A little knot of ironclad men gathered about the three standards – the Cross of the Holy Religion, the banner of St. John the Baptist, and the banner of Our Lady. They were marvellous things, these banners, embroidered in coloured silks by devout nuns, and they made a brave show flying above the smoke and murk of the battle against a blue sky.

Janissaries and Sipahis were now pouring through the breach, so close packed that they impeded each other's advance and offered a terribly easy target to the archers and hand-gunners behind the retrenchment and on the wall of Provence. The fight on the wall around the base of the tower of Italy went on. The walk-way was narrow, and D'Aubusson says that they were fighting chest to chest. The press was so thick that the archers and hand-gunners in the occupied tower dared not fire for fear of killing their own men, and soon a gallant band of Knights forced their way into the tower and slaughtered the occupants. The crescent of the Ottomans was hurled to the ground.

The breach was filling up with dead, and screaming men were falling from the wall. But some did manage to get down alive into the town, killing Rhodians and Jews before they themselves, cut off from their fellows, were surrounded and disposed of at some cost to the defenders.

D'Aubusson's armour was red with blood – some of it his own from four flesh wounds – when a gigantic Janissary thrust a spear clean through his breastplate into the right side of his chest, puncturing a lung. As he was being carried down from the wall he heard a great shout go up from the Turks and saw that the men in the breach had turned to run and were hacking their way through the advancing ranks of their comrades on the 'hogs-back'.

Panic fear had seized them. The Janissaries did their best, cutting down the retreating Bashi Bazouks and attempting to rally the waverers; but they too were killed by frantic, terror-stricken deserters. The garrison now left their retrenchments and hurried down from the battlements to join the pursuit. Led by Antoine D'Aubusson (the Captain General), the Admiral Piozzasco, Fabrizio Del Carretto, the victor of St. Nicholas, and the flower of chivalry from Provence, Anjou, Dijon, Perigord,

*D' Aubusson leads the defence of the breach near
the Tower of Italy, from a woodcut of 1496*

Paris and Verona, Germany, England, Ireland and Scotland, Castile, Aragon and Leon, the defenders flung themselves like a pack of hounds upon the fleeing Ottomans. The struggle had now become a massacre. The Turks were mowed down like sheep or, as Caoursin has it, 'like swine'. They were pursued far beyond the advance batteries into their camp on the slopes of Mount St. Stephen, where the gold and silver standard of the Sultan was captured. At last, sated with slaughter, the Christians returned to the city, bearing the Ottoman standard, and every pike decorated with a Turkish head.

Porter is a little censorious of what he describes as 'the credulity of our forefathers'. 'Contemporaries,' he says, 'record that at the most critical moment, when the Grand Master was surrounded and well-nigh overcome by his assailants there appeared in the Heavens a refulgent Cross of gold, by the side of which stood a beautiful woman, clothed in garments of dazzling white, a lance in her hand, and a buckler on her arm, accompanied by a man dressed in goatskins and followed by a band of heavenly warriors, armed with flaming swords . . . a ready credence was easily gained from the pious but ignorant multitudes of those times, it soon became established that the safety of Rhodes was due to the personal and visible interposition of the Blessed Virgin Mary, and the patron saint of the Order, St. John the Baptist, supported for the occasion by a chosen band of the celestial host.'

It may be – whatever our view of the probability of super-natural intervention – that the panic amongst the Ottoman irregulars went to the root of one of the several causes of Misac's failure. There were too many Christians, or conscript apostates in his army: Greeks whose distaste for the Latins did not go so far as to make them forget their Christianity; Albanians, Serbs, Ukranians and Macedonians. The vision of the three banners on the skyline had only to trigger a pang of Christian conscience, and the waverer soon became a menace to his fellows. Panic followed.

Caoursin gives figures of the Turkish casualties: 3,500 Turks were slain, he says, in the breach and in the retreat. 300 Janissaries who had irrupted into the Jews' Quarter and had been cut off were also slain. 'There were corpses all over the city, on the walls, in the ditch, in the enemy stockades and in the sea . . . they had to be burned to avoid an infectious sickness.' De Curti and Pantaleone say 3,000. D'Aubusson, himself, says 3,500, of whom 300 were slain in the fight in the Jews' Quarter. All these figures are highly suspect; but there is no doubt that the slaughter was convincing to the enemy.

Caoursin is moved by the association of the Jews' Quarter to a biblical eulogy of D'Aubusson and his Knights, who fought 'as in ancient times the glorious Maccabees fought for their faith and for the liberty of the Jewish people'.

As to the defenders' casualties, the figures are doubtless as heavily underestimated as the enemy's losses are multiplied. D'Aubusson reported that 'many of our Knights and Bailiffs fell, fighting to the last wherever the combat was thickest. We and others of our comrades sustained many wounds. . . .' De Curti asks us to believe that in the fight for the Jews' Quarter the Order lost twenty killed, of whom ten were Knights, 'including the Bailiff of Germany'. King gives the following English casualties: Thomas Benn – Bailiff of Egle, John Wakelyn – Commander of Carbrooke, Henry Hales – Commander of Baddesford, Thomas Plumpton, Adam Tedbond, Henry Battesby and Henry Anlaby, all killed. Marmaduke Lumley (later Grand Prior of Ireland) was seriously wounded but recovered. Those who appear to have survived unhurt were: John Boswell (a Scot), Leonard Tybert, Walter Westborough and John Roche (an Irishman).

Misac Palaeologos Pasha apparently took no personal part in the fighting – not even when his emperor's standard was in peril. His high hopes and his promises to the Sultan of an easy victory had been shattered in a fight which had lasted no more than two hours. His total losses during a campaign of less than three months amounted, we are told by the Christian chroniclers, to 9,000 dead and 15,000 wounded. Making allowance for sickness and disease – we have only to recall the dysentery and the trench fever of more modern armies to imagine the casualties which these things, and worse, might have caused in a fifteenth-century army – we may accept that Misac lost at least a quarter of his army. No precise figure is possible.

As to the Christian losses: the Grand Master himself was at

first thought to be dying; but he was immensely tough and had some of the best physicians in the world. We know that Fra Johan von Aue,[21] the Saxon Grand Prior of Germany was killed, and that of fourteen English, Scottish and Irish Knights whose names survive, seven were killed and at least one badly wounded.[22] Altogether, 231 Knights who were sufficiently notable for Caoursin, De Curti or Pantaleone to notice, are said to have died – almost half the total of Knights given by Caoursin; and to these must be added the nameless Servants-at-Arms, the common soldiery, the sailors, the Rhodian militia and the civilians. Sickness must also have taken its toll of the garrison.

The city, the Grand Master's palace, many churches, the proud Tower of St. Nicholas, the wall and the tower of Italy, were in ruins. A large part of the rest of the defences was badly damaged. The countryside had been scorched and devastated – first by the Rhodians themselves and then by the retreating Turks, who uprooted trees and grapevines, and slew every living creature in their path. It would take months, even years, to restore the damage. But the Holy Religion was unconquered and in being. The white cross of St. John on its scarlet field still flew over the ruins.

The Ottomans took ten days to strike camp, collect their wounded and their impedimenta, and embark their whole force – though they left behind 'ropes for tying up prisoners and a great quantity of stakes for tormenting the living, having decided to impale all the men and women over ten years of age[23] and to carry off into slavery those of more tender years, forcing them to apostatize'.

Perhaps an opportunity was missed of harrying the last of the besiegers as they took off from the beach at Trianda on 7th August; but the garrison was tired. As the final squadron was making off eastwards towards Marmarice in the late afternoon, a sudden squall blew up from the south-west, and the delighted Rhodians saw, driving before it, a carrack and a brigantine flying the flags of the Pope and King Ferdinand of Naples. Pope Sixtus IV (Francesco della Rovere) had been General of the Franciscans and a great preacher. The Franciscans were strong in Rhodes and had performed prodigies. Sixtus has been stigmatized as a shameless worldling – patron of Botticelli, Ghirlandaio,

Perugino and Pinturicchio, patron of the Vatican Library, builder of the Sistine Chapel, and cynical approver of the Spanish Inquisition. Yet it was he who had persuaded Naples to send a ship to Rhodes and sent one himself. It was more than the rest of Christendom could spare. The Turks, who had heard stories that France, Naples and Rome were all sending aid to the Order, feared that these two vessels were the advance pickets of a Christian armada. They detached a force of galleys[24] to deal with them. The carrack, the *Santa Maria*, was heavily armed for her time, with long-range culverins mounted in the waist. She raked the Turks repeatedly and drove them off. The brigantine, less fortunate, was unable to make the galley port in the squall. A lucky shot carried away her mainmast and she was driven, willy-nilly, towards the Turks; but the *Santa Maria*, commanded by one Juan Poo, a Biscayan from Asturias, covered her. The squall blew itself out by nightfall and the relief force, laden with welcome victuals and a body of fresh, well-armed troops, entered harbour, their companies marvelling no doubt at the ruin and the devastation of the city. In the *Santa Maria*, bearing letters to D'Aubusson from the Holy Father and the King of Naples, was the envoy Francesco Aversano. He was brought before D'Aubusson where he lay – dying as was supposed – in the Hospital.

Sixtus IV had written that if within fifteen days D'Aubusson had not reported the end of the siege, he would send a great many ships and men and for a cause so sacred as the defence of Rhodes he would willingly empty the Papal treasury. The Holy Father probably meant what he wrote; but D'Aubusson may be forgiven if he murmured: 'We have implored your help. We have been answered with words. . . .'

Misac and his army hung about Marmarice for another eleven days, almost as if they feared to go home. Turkish authorities blame Misac for the failure, charging him with avarice in reserving to himself and the Sultan all the fruits of a victory, instead of announcing that the traditional three days' pillage would be permitted. We may, perhaps, be more charitable to him and suppose that he wished to avoid a wholesale massacre of his fellow Greeks. His repeated attempts to persuade the Grand

Master to a compromised peace also show him in a not unfavourable light – as a man, if not as a soldier.

Mehmet was furious. He condemned Misac to death, relenting before sentence could be carried out – mollified, perhaps, by the news of Ahmed Keduk's conquest of Otranto; and immediately began to mobilize a new army and to refit the fleet for a fresh descent upon Rhodes which he would lead in person.

Misac Palaeologos not only escaped with his life. He was not even beaten insensible – a minor punishment in the Sultan's scale of penalties. He was exiled to Gallipoli and, restored to favour in his old age, he was sent to govern Egypt by the Sultan Selim the Grim.

Mehmet's new army was not ready until the following year (the season was too late for another campaign in 1480); but in April 1481 he set out to march across Asia Minor. He had got as far as Nicomedia, fifty miles from Constantinople, on 3rd May, when he died suddenly, probably of dysentery. He was forty-nine. His sons Bajazet and Djem immediately began to dispute the succession and there was no one to lead a new attack on those 'most damnable of the Kuffar, sons of Error and allies of Sheitan . . .'[25] the Knights of Rhodes.

5

THE YEARS OF POWER
1481–1521

The years between the two sieges of 1480 and 1522 spanned some of the most momentous years in the history of western civilization. They included the discovery of the New World, the closing by the Ottomans, in 1511, of the old, land trade routes to the Far East, and the opening of the new sea routes by the seamen of Portugal; the full flowering and the spread of the Italian Renaissance, and the explosion of the German–Swiss Reformation.

The chief quality of these years was their tremendous energy: energy which seemed to many, and not least to the garrisons of Rhodes and its dependencies, to be misdirected. The victory of 1480 raised D'Aubusson's personal prestige, as well as that of the Holy Religion, to a height unprecedented in the history of the Order. The Rhodians, too, shared in this prestige. William Caoursin, the Rhodian Vice-Chancellor, was sent as ambassador to the Papal court. The Rhodians were excused taxation for five years. Gifts came from all over Europe. Merchants and adventurers flocked to the island. But D'Aubusson was not complacent. He began at once the restoration of the ruined city and the erection of new and better defences. He kept his promise to the Franciscans and built them a monastery. On the site of the battle for the Jews' Quarter he erected a new church dedicated to Our Lady of Victories. He further ensured the continuance of the *guerre de course* by building and chartering new vessels for the fleet. A Genoese corsair, Francisco Mego, was given a 'perpetual safe conduct' to exercise the *Corso* against Islam wherever its ships might be found, using Rhodes as his base.[1] And in 1481, when the Mamelukes had infringed the terms of the current truce, a naval force was sent to harass shipping and make raids along the coasts of Egypt and Syria.

The dynastic quarrel of Mehmet's two sons made any further

Turkish attack improbable in the immediate future, and the Order entered a phase of strangely reversed relations with Constantinople – in which the Ottomans virtually became the tributaries of Rhodes. The central figure of this bizarre period was the pretender Djem, third son of the Sultan Mehmet.[2] Mustafa, the eldest, had been strangled by his father's order as a penalty for conducting a love affair with a wife of the Vezir Achmet. Bajazet, the second son, had been born before Mehmet's accession. Djem's claim to the throne was based on his being *porphyrogenitus* (born in the purple; after his father's accession)[3] and relied on Byzantine tradition. This contention might be sound in regard to the throne of Constantinople; but not in respect of the Ottoman ancestral lands, where the succession would belong by Islamic tradition to the eldest surviving male descendant of Othman. Bajazet, who enjoyed the support of the Janissaries and of the able soldier Achmet, was proclaimed in Constantinople and Djem at Brusa. An army led by Bajazet with Achmet as his chief-of-staff defeated Djem at Brusa, and early in 1482 the pretender fled to Egypt. He failed to enlist the Mamelukes in his cause, but was more successful with the vassal Emir of Caramania, whose help he accepted on his return from a pilgrimage to Mecca. Again defeated by Achmet, Djem took to the mountains, and bethought himself of his old acquaintance D'Aubusson, with whom he had had some dealings as ambassador for his father, and for whom he seems to have entertained respect and affection. He dispatched a messenger secretly to Rhodes asking for the protection of the Order.

The possible advantages to be gained by the entertainment of so embarrassing a guest – who still had a considerable following in the Ottoman domains – were as evident as the perils. Djem remained a potential threat to the Turks and the Order might elect to exploit him; but Bajazet might strike first to remove the threat. The Order's honour was involved once the Hospitallers had promised their protection, and Djem must come to no harm while in their care. In Rhodes it would not be easy to protect him from the long arm of his brother's vengeance. D'Aubusson consulted with the Council, and after some dispute it was agreed to dispatch a safe conduct to Djem, who was then able to make his way to Alanya (ancient Coracesium) in the Gulf of Antalya on the coast of Caramania. There the Prior of Castile, Don Alvarez de Zuñiga, met him with an escort and carried him in the Order's carrack to the relative safety of the Convent, where he arrived on 29th July 1482.

Djem was received with imperial honours. 'A bridge eighteen feet in length, covered with rich tapestry, was thrown out into the harbour to enable him to land on horseback.'[4] In his imperial robes and bejewelled turban, escorted by the Prior of Castile and a company of Spanish Knights, Djem was greeted by the Grand Master and the Conventual Bailiffs, magnificently mounted as the occasion demanded, and wearing their black capes with the eight-pointed white Cross of the Holy Religion over their damascened parade armour. The kiss of peace was exchanged and the cavalcade set off to parade slowly through the streets of the city, which were hung with garlands and evergreens as for a feast day. They were crowded too with wondering, applauding Rhodian citizens, Venetian and Genoese and Florentine, English and French and Flemish merchants, and seamen from all over Europe and North Africa. Rich tapestries hung from every balcony, and the bold, unveiled Christian women leaned provocatively over to catch a better view and to throw flowers in the path of this young Sultan, son of the terrifying Mehmet, and descendant of the race of conquerors whom they feared more than Satan himself. The women were probably disappointed, for he was physically unprepossessing, with a twisted nose and a squint: of middle height, very broad, and with unusually long arms. But Djem, a true Turk, remarked that 'it was with great justice that the Rhodians were considered the loveliest women in Asia'.

At last the cavalcade passed through the Gate of St. Anthony into the Convent, and Djem commenced his tragic exile.

He was treated as an honoured guest. D'Aubusson exerted all his charm – that charm which 'easily captured the friendship of anyone who met him and whose affection he studied to win'. Hunting, coursing and hawking parties, tourneys, spectacles and feasts worthy of his rank were organized – like so many of the race of Othman, the young pretender was no stranger to the wine cup. But always there were three or four armed Knights at his elbow. His food and his drink were tasted before he was allowed to touch either. He was never alone. Yet he seems to have been happy in Rhodes and to have grown genuinely fond of D'Aubusson.

We shall never know all the considerations which prompted the actors in this strange little drama, from which few of the Christian characters emerge with anything but discredit. Caoursin, a loyal servant of the Order, and another captive of D'Aubusson's charm, offers every kind of explanation for the conduct of the Grand Master; but enemies of the Order have seen him as a willing party to a squalid scheme for using Djem to the limit of his bargaining value against Bajazet and, finally, as an accessory in his murder. Caoursin says that it was on Djem's own initiative that he left Rhodes: an initiative with which the Grand Master and Council, after some deliberation, fell in the more readily because of persistent rumours and agents' reports of plots to dispose of Djem. Rhodes was too near Bajazet. In the mother house of D'Aubusson's Langue at Bourgeneuf – within the family demesne of La Marche – he could be more effectively protected.

It seems that the decision to send him to France had already been reached – though Djem was still in Rhodes – when, in late August of 1482, an embassy from Constantinople, dispatched by Achmet Pasha, arrived with proposals for a 'durable peace'. Arrangements were made for plenipotentiaries of the Order to return to Constantinople to negotiate.[5]

On 1st September 1482 Djem sailed with an escort in the great carrack. His parting from D'Aubusson was charged with emotion. We are told that 'forgetting the proud reserve of his Asiatic nature . . . Djem fell at D'Aubusson's feet in a paroxysm of grief, bathing them in tears . . . while the calm, fearless, intrepid D'Aubusson wept upon the neck of Djem tears of paternal affection'.

Djem left three documents with D'Aubusson.[6] The first appointed the Order to treat on his behalf with his brother, the Sultan, to secure whatever terms they could, and to obtain from him such pension or tribute as would cover the cost of his entertainment. The second document declared that he left Rhodes of his own wish and by no compulsion of the Order. The third was a very extraordinary declaration, binding Djem and his heirs and successors, should he ever retrieve the throne of the Ottomans, to eternal friendship for the Order:

Know all men, that I, the Sultan Djem, sprung from the Ottoman race, son of the invincible Mehmet, king of kings, and Sovereign Emperor of Greece and Asia, am infinitely indebted to the very generous and most illustrious prince Seigneur Pierre D'Aubusson, Grand Master of Rhodes; but know also that, considering the kind offices which he has rendered me in the most fateful adventure of my life, and desirous of marking my gratitude as far as the present state of my fortunes will permit, I promise solemnly to God and our great Prophet, that if ever I recover, either entirely or in part, my father's Imperial crown, I promise and swear that I will maintain a constant peace, and an inviolable friendship, with the Grand Master D'Aubusson, and with all his successors, in accordance with the following articles. In the first place, I pledge myself, my children, and my children's children to maintain a perpetual attachment for the Order of St. John of Jerusalem, to the extent that neither I myself, nor my children, shall ever do an injury to the Knights, either by land or by sea, so that far from obstructing their vessels, or disturbing the commerce of the merchants of Rhodes, or of the other islands of the Religion, we will open our ports to them, and will permit them to enter freely into all the provinces under our sway, as though they were themselves our subjects; or rather we will treat them as our friends, in permitting them to buy and sell, and to transport their merchandise wherever they may think fit, without the payment of any duty or tax. In addition to this, I consent that the Grand Master shall withdraw every year from my dominions 300 Christians of both sexes, and of such ages that he may select, to transfer them to the island of the Order, or for any other purpose which he may think advisable; and in order to make some return for the outlay which the Grand Master has made, and is making every day, with such liberality on my account, I agree to pay him in specie the sum of 150,000 gold crowns. Lastly, I promise upon oath to restore to him all the islands, all the lands, and all the fortresses which the Ottoman emperors have captured from the Order; and in testimony that such is my will I have signed this deed with my hand, and have sealed it with my seal. Done at Rhodes, in the palace of the Auberge de France, on the 5th day of the month of Reget, in the year of the Hegira 337 [31st August 1482].

Djem had scarcely reached France when the terms of the treaty with Bajazet were sealed (and dated 8th December 1482). The Order was to receive indefinitely an annual compensation of 10,000 gold ducats for the damage caused by the attack of 1480. A further sum of 35,000 Venetian ducats was to be paid annually to the Order for the subsistence of Djem (it was duly and regularly paid after he left the Convent). As for the rest, there were mutual expressions of regard and promises of non-aggression which neither side can have expected to last indefinitely.

Djem had hopes of persuading the French king, and perhaps other western princes, to support an attempt to unseat Bajazet; but the princes were not enthusiastic. If they could keep Bajazet quiet – he was apparently not belligerently inclined – they would be free to pursue their own endless feuds.

When ambassadors from Djem, now established at Bourgeneuf, reached the court of Charles VIII, they were coldly received. That eccentric monarch was busy with his plans for possessing himself of Naples, and had not yet appreciated the pretender's potential as a hostage. For the next six years Djem remained under the protection of the Order, guarded day and night. And then Pope Innocent VIII saw an opportunity of gaining some advantage from the possession of the young pretender's person. This Genoese Pope (Gianbattista Cibo), who reigned from 1484 to 1492, was yet another of the renaissance pontiffs who fell into the error of behaving like Italian princes rather than as the heads of the Universal Church which they were. Having achieved a large illegitimate family before taking orders, he had good reason to become adept at patronage and nepotism. His exactions and his sales of benefices, including those of the Order of Rhodes, scandalized even his Italian contemporaries. Far from aiding or encouraging others to aid the Order, he was Turcophil by inclination and received (in 1490) the first Turkish embassy ever to arrive in Rome. He ordered D'Aubusson to hand Djem over. The Grand Master demurred: the Order had guaranteed his safety. D'Aubusson could not say so; but he distrusted his spiritual overlord. Not for the first or the last time, the Holy

Religion was torn between the duty of obedience to Rome, and her own honour. The alternative to obedience was open rebellion, and rebellion would wound Mother Church even more grievously than her unworthy pontiffs had already done. It might also destroy the Order. Advised by the Council, D'Aubusson surrendered Djem.

Djem arrived in Rome in March 1488, and was received with splendid ceremony. Innocent showed his gratitude by solemnly declaring that no more alienations of the Order's property, or improper appointments to its dignities, would be made. He also merged the decrepit Orders of the Holy Sepulchre and St. Lazarus under the banner of the Hospital – a left-handed gift, since the two Orders were bankrupt.

Unhappily for his reputation, D'Aubusson had accepted a Cardinal's hat from Innocent in 1485. It was in fact no more than an automatic honour attaching to his appointment as Papal Legate in the East; but the preferment – if preferment it was – together with the concessions made by Innocent in 1488, have been unjustly read as the price of Djem's betrayal.

The pretender was treated well by Innocent, who now received a pension regularly from Bajazet for the young hostage's entertainment. Porter says that life was very different for Djem after the election of Alexander VI (Rodrigo Borgia, 1492–1503), whose pontificate is notorious. He had no interest in the Hospitallers save as a source of revenue, or as a means of exerting pressure on the Sultan at no cost to himself. He dismissed Djem's bodyguard of Knights of St. John and 'locked him up in the grim castle of St. Angelo'. But John Burchard, a German born in Strasbourg, who was Master of Ceremonies to five Popes between 1483 and 1506, and kept a careful diary, says that Alexander, like his predecessor, treated Djem as an honoured guest:

... though Djem was not allowed to leave Rome, yet Alexander VI and his sons treated the Turkish Prince in very friendly and courteous fashion. He moved about the city with an escort and was accorded an honourable place in all ceremonial functions. Don Juan Borgia in particular appeared to cultivate him and frequently dressed in the style of a Turk when accompanying Djem on his journeys through Rome. . . .[7]

As to the bodyguard, it is true that the Knights appointed by

D'Aubusson were dismissed; but a token participation by the Order in Djem's affairs seems to have been retained, for, when Djem was produced for the inspection of Bajazet's ambassador at the splendid ceremonies in June 1493, he was accompanied by a Knight of Rhodes who was a brother of Cardinal Giovanni Borgia.[8] Bajazet had directed his ambassador to 'commit his beloved brother Djem to the Pontiff's care so that his detention should lack nothing for his comfort'.[9]

In September 1494 Charles VIII of France, an unbalanced, though brave hunchback, invaded Italy. Ludovico Sforza, the ruler of Milan, welcomed him. The powerful della Rovere and Colonna factions joined him, and Savonarola hailed him as the saviour of Florence.

This French adventure seems to have been initiated by nothing more noble than a perverted desire on the part of Charles and his young chivalry to emulate the crusading exploits of their ancestors in a more comfortable environment, and to 'save' Italy from Spain by means of a 'cavalcade in glittering armour under the blue Italian sky, riding across a beautiful land'. Venice remained neutral. Alexander VI was deserted by many of his own people, and Ferdinand of Spain and the Emperor Maximilian did nothing to help him. By January 1495 the French were in effective control of Rome and the Papal States. Alexander retired to the relative security of St. Angelo, keeping Djem with him, which may explain Porter's assertion that the pretender was imprisoned in the fortress. He commenced a series of typically tortuous negotiations with Charles, in which the Frenchman was far from having everything his own way.

On 11th January 1495 it was agreed to hand Djem over to the custody of Charles for a period of six months. It does not appear that Charles had any specific use for Djem at this time; but the control of his person was a valuable insurance, at least during a period in which he looked forward to securing his Italian conquests, undisturbed by papal intrigues. The French king was to pay the Pope 20,000 ducats, and give security in Florentine bonds for the return of the pretender within six months. There was also to be an exchange of sureties in the shape of a number of nobles, lords and prelates.

Meanwhile, Don Giorgio Bucciardo, the Pope's envoy to the Sultan, had been captured near Florence in November, on his return journey from Constantinople, by Giovanni della Rovere. Bucciardo was carrying gold, and, it was said, a letter from Bajazet to the Pope which was given wide publicity after the death of Djem. The letter, which was very possibly a forgery, read:

> Sultan Bajazet Khan, son of Sultan Mahomet Khan, by the Grace of God, Emperor and Lord of Asia, Europe and all Seas, to the Father and Lord of all Christians by Divine Providence, Alexander VI, worthy Pontiff of the Roman Church. . . . Amongst other things, Don Giorgio told us how the French King is eager to seize Djem, Our brother, at present in Your Highness's keeping, and this would be an act much against Our wish, bringing great harm to Your Highness and injury to all your Christian peoples. We have therefore reached an agreement with Don Giorgio for the peace, aid and honour of Your Greatness and also for Our satisfaction. It would be good, we judge, that the original sentence of death on Our brother Djem, who is held in Your Highness's hands, should be carried out, for this would be a release into life for him, useful for Your Authority and most convenient and gratifying to Our position. If Your Magnificence is agreeable to please Us in this matter, and indeed we trust that you will be prudent to be so, then for your greater security, and Our deeper satisfaction, you should execute the deed as quickly as possible. Thereby Your Highness will be the better pleased and Djem will be more quickly delivered from the straits of this world so that his soul will have peace in the next. Furthermore, if Your Highness will undertake to fulfil this agreement, and will command that Djem's body shall be delivered to us at any point on Our coasts, We Sultan Bajazet Khan promise to hand over 300,000 Ducats at any place pleasing to Your Eminence with which sum you may buy possessions for your sons. . . .[10]

The letter ends with assurances of deep and lasting friendship, and promises by Bajazet never to 'harm any Christian by land or sea . . . except such as mean to harm Us or our subjects', and is dated 15th September 1494 'according to the Coming of Christ'.

On 29th January 1495, Djem was escorted from St. Angelo to the Palazzo Venezia and handed over to Charles. Cesare Borgia – himself a hostage for papal good behaviour – accompanied the march south towards Naples.

What happened next is obscure. Caoursin says that Djem became ill at Terracina, just south of the Pontine Marshes. Porter says that he was already suffering from the effects of a delayed-action venom from the wide selection of such weapons in the Borgia armoury. Burchard recorded: 'We learned on February 25th that Prince Djem had died in the Castel Capuana in Naples through eating or drinking something unsuitable for him.' Parker remarks that Burchard was 'deliberately vague or reticent in describing some events such as the death of the Turkish Prince Djem'.

Cesare Borgia had escaped from Charles's surveillance on 30th January, disguised as an ostler, after the cavalcade reached Velletri – but before Djem had reached Terracina.

Djem's body, and all his household, were sent to Bajazet, who 'paid handsomely for the safe delivery of the Corpse', according to Pauli.[11] But Pauli does not say who received the money and the statement has little value as evidence.

The true circumstances of Djem's death are beyond our reach. There is no proof that Alexander or his son Cesare actually had Djem murdered – or murdered him themselves. The Turk could have died of any one of a dozen undiagnosed, natural ailments which looked like poisoning; or the poisoning might easily have been effected by an agent of Bajazet without any complicity on Alexander's or Cesare's part. But Alexander's reputation is against him and Cesare certainly had both motive and opportunity. Poison was a popular political weapon: Henry VIII tried to have Cardinal Pole poisoned during the Council of Trent. However, Bouhours says that 'the partisans of the Roman Court asserted that the Turkish Prince so gave himself over to his pleasures during the first days of his liberty that he died of excessive debauchery', and that 'there were those who said that the Venetians corrupted by Turkish money and alarmed by the French expedition caused Djem to be secretly poisoned'.

The importance to Rhodes of this sad and tortuous little drama was the breathing space which the living pretender had given to the Order in which to repair the ravages of 1480, and to recoup some of the treasure expended on the defence. When Djem was surrendered to the Pope, eight years of uneasy peace with Bajazet had been bought.

Caoursin's lengthy apology for D'Aubusson might suggest that the Order was not without some part in the intrigues which followed the surrender.[12] However, it has never been seriously contended by any unbiased authority that D'Aubusson connived at Djem's murder. It is scarcely possible to see any motive for it. Apart from matters of honour, Djem alive was always more valuable to the Order than Djem dead. Even after he had passed into papal control he was a bargaining counter in dealings with the Sultan, and in the unlikely event of his recovering his father's dominions 'either wholly or in part', the Order stood to gain even more than it had from the treaty with Bajazet.

The two crucial decisions for which D'Aubusson and his Council were responsible were first to allow Djem to leave Rhodes and second to hand him over to the Pope. If we are to believe Caoursin, Djem wanted to leave, and it can certainly be argued that he was safer from Bajazet in Bourgneuf than in Rhodes, though he was also more vulnerable subsequently to papal pressure. The Order's original guarantee went no further than 'tutus aditus exitusque' and it was fulfilled. D'Aubusson would have appreciated the possibility of Djem becoming a pawn in European politics and how remote were the chances of a 'crusade' in Djem's interest (he never deserted Islam). None the less, it was reasonable to allow Djem freedom for his own manœuvring and preferable to keeping him in Rhodes against his wish.

The transfer of Djem to Innocent deserves censure much more. But the unhappy fact is that D'Aubusson and the Council had no other choices than assent or an open rupture with the Papacy, and the Order would never go to that extreme. It might be said in mitigation that Djem was well-treated by Innocent, but the transfer also exposed him to Alexander and Charles. Once he was in the Pope's custody the Order's influence over what happened to him was very limited, and so was their direct responsibility. But the Council must have known the consequences of a surrender and their decision, though perhaps inevitable, was to that extent culpable.

In Europe the balance of power was momentarily shifting towards Spain. In 1492 the little Muslim state of Granada, last foothold of Islam in western Europe – but no longer the Islam of the Jihad, rather a harmless centre of learning and luxury – fell to Spanish arms and confirmed Spanish nationhood.

In 1495 Charles VIII of France found himself deserted by his Italian allies, who resented the plundering and rapine of the German and Swiss mercenaries who comprised a large part of his army. After a technical victory at Fornovo, he escaped homewards.

The Knights of the Spanish Langues in the Convent at Rhodes became more arrogant than ever, and more resentful of the French majority. At about this time the fateful name of one Andrea D'Amaral appeared in the roll of the Langue of Castile.

Bajazet had continued to court the Holy Religion after Djem's departure for Europe. In 1487 an embassy from Constantinople, led by Cariati Bey, arrived bearing the Holy Relic of the Right Hand of St. John in a sumptuous reliquary. But the peace was uneasy. Only the worsening relations between the Ottomans and the Mamelukes, and the ever-present menace of the Shi-ite Persians to the east kept Bajazet's warlike Vezirs from attacking Rhodes. In 1488 open war at sea broke out between the Turks and the Egyptians, extending the breathing space for Rhodes by another two years; but the Order had not been at pains to control the activities of corsairs operating from Rhodes, and when Djem died in 1495 D'Aubusson knew that a Turkish attack could not be long delayed.

The archives relate his efforts to prepare for it. He sent Fra Paola di Saloma to Sicily to invite 'vessels of every nation and condition whose owners and masters wish to espouse the sacred cause of war against the Infidels . . . to repair to Rhodes where they would find sanctuary and safe conduct'.[13] It was something very like piracy. In 1496 the fine new Boulevard of Auvergne was completed. It was the first true bastion to be built anywhere, specially designed by the Florentine engineer Di Giorgio, and embodying all the latest experience of the Italian Wars.

In 1499 Rhodes was visited by the plague; but the Order did not apparently suffer greatly. In the same year the Ottomans attacked Venice, landing an army near the city at Friuli (Santa Margherita). They were repulsed; but the Order had shown its hand by furnishing a contingent to help the Venetians, and in 1500 the Pope, frightened by Turkish arms on Italian soil, declared a crusade. He appointed D'Aubusson Captain General of the Holy League, in which France, Spain, Portugal, Venice, the Papacy and the Order were allied. No one did anything except the Order and Venice, whose fleets concentrated at Paros – the Religion furnishing four great ships and four galleys. The great carrack, anchored at Paros and intended as the maintenance ship for the Christian fleet, is said by Bosio[14] to have been 'almost like a Granary or Storehouse capable of meeting all the needs of an armada'. The Captain General of the Galleys was the Englishman Thomas Docwra. But the promised squadrons of the Papacy, Spain and Portugal did not arrive and the French were recalled while on passage.

In 1502 the Papal squadron arrived, commanded by the Latin Bishop of Paphos. D'Aubusson had resigned his command of the League's forces to the Admiral of the Order, Fra Ludovico di Scalenghe. Several carracks laden with rich merchandise from Chios for Constantinople fell prey to the galleys of the Order, as did five Turkish galeotts brought to action off Samos. On 29th August 1502 the forces of the League occupied Santa Maura. In 1503 the Venetians made peace, and the Order was committed, alone now, to war with Bajazet: a prospect by which they were undismayed.

On 30th June 1503 Pierre D'Aubusson died. He was eighty. His reign of twenty-seven years had carried the Holy Religion from the depths of peril to heights of power and renown towards which friends and enemies alike lifted their eyes with a fearful awe as to 'creatures more than human'.

The new Grand Master was Emeric D'Amboise, Grand Prior of the Langue of France. The death of Pope Alexander VI, shortly after the Grand Master's election, spared D'Amboise some of the anxieties which had clouded D'Aubusson's last years, though new ones took their place. Bajazet had now made peace with the Mamelukes, and D'Amboise had to tread delicately to avoid bringing the combined weight of the two great Muslim powers about his ears. Pope Julius II (Giuliano della Rovere, 1503–1513), whose military virtues ought to have endeared the Knights to him, nevertheless looked jealously at the Order's properties as a means of paying for his military adventures.

He was a nephew of Sixtus IV, and also a Franciscan. By contrast with Alexander he was a paragon of virtue; but he dreamed of a united Italy, and tried to drive the French and Spaniards out of the peninsula. He was also a great hawker of benefices, and his courage and intelligence better fitted the helmeted head of a soldier than the tonsure of a Franciscan. Erasmus wrote, openly: 'How, O Bishop standing in the room of the Apostles, dare you teach the peoples the things that pertain to war?'[15] And the voice of Erasmus was only one of the many voices raised against the failure of the Church to reform herself. The Holy Religion was in the unhappy position of sharing the stigma of the Papacy which was selling her benefices.

In August 1503 sixteen Turkish galleys raided the coast of Rhodes, sacking coastal villages and sending raiding parties inland. As the fleet retired northwards, they were brought to action by the galleys of the Holy Religion commanded by Don Diego Almeida, Grand Prior of Portugal. Eight Turks were sunk and two captured. Unhappily, a careless gunner, dropping a match into a powder keg, blew the bows off one of the triremes of the Order, killing eight Knights and six sailors.[16] On 16th November the Council voted a replacement, deeming it necessary 'for the reputation of the Religion with Infidels and with the Faithful' that there should not be less than three triremes in commission.[17]

A Turkish squadron which approached Leros was scared off by the simple stratagem of lining the battlements of the under-manned fort with peasants and their women dressed in the red surcoats of the Order.[18]

In the autumn of 1506, two galleys of the Order encountered seven fustae of the Mamelukes, bent on the plunder of Kos, and captured all seven, taking their crews prisoner and releasing many Christian slaves. In 1507, the great carrack of the Order, cruising near Candia, came upon the Mamelukes' great ship *Mogarbina*, and, after a sharp action, she fell, scarcely damaged, to the Order. She was the Egyptian treasure ship and made regular voyages between Alexandria and the Barbary Coast laden with valuable merchandise – a rich prize indeed. Rossi says that the capture was 'the most notable ever made by the Navy of the Order, both in respect of the number of prisoners taken, many of whom were ransomed for a great price, and for the value of the captured merchandise'.[19] Shortly after this success, the victors of Kos took three smaller Egyptian ships off the south coast of Cyprus.

In 1510 the Order achieved the greatest sea victory of its Rhodes period at Laiazzo (Ayas), near Alexandretta.[20] The Sultan Bajazet and the Mameluke Sultan Quansuh al-Guri had decided upon a combined effort to confront the Portuguese in the Red Sea and Indian Ocean, where the Portuguese were successfully engaged in capturing the immensely lucrative spice trade as well as other rich commerce of the East Indies. The Mamelukes had set up a base at Laiazzo whence they replenished their shipbuilding timber, and in the summer of 1510 the Order's agents reported a large convoy, commanded by the nephew of Quansuh, on passage for Laiazzo. A strong force sailed from Rhodes on 6th August. The French L'Isle Adam commanded the 'ships' – that is to say, in the loose terminology of the time, the vessels relying primarily on sail power. The Portuguese Andrea D'Amaral commanded the galleys, with their oars as main power, and was senior officer of the combined squadron. A bitter quarrel between the two took place when they neared Laiazzo.

It was nearing the end of August, when the winds are changeable, and L'Isle Adam questioned the wisdom of entering the anchorage with his lumbering, unhandy sailing vessels, where he might be be-calmed or blown under the guns of shore-based batteries by an on-shore wind. The impetuous D'Amaral was for a dash at the anchored Mameluke timber fleet. In the event L'Isle Adam's prudence prevailed and was entirely justified by the resounding victory which followed.

It was the Mamelukes who were imprudent. They came out to meet the Knights in the open sea, and, after the exchange of a few rounds of cannon fire, the ships and the galleys of Rhodes grappled their opponents and boarded. The Mamelukes fought and died gallantly – amongst them the Sultan's nephew – but the slaughter was too much for the survivors, and at last they surrendered. In all, eleven great ships and four galleys were captured by the Knights. They then landed parties who chased the shore garrison inland, setting fire to the stocks of timber awaiting shipment. On passage to Rhodes they fell in with friendly craft who reported a combined Turkish and Egyptian fleet southward bound from Gallipoli. Battle-scarred and hampered by their prizes, navigating with skeleton prize crews and full of prisoners, the Knights wisely avoided an encounter and reached Rhodes safely.

It is tempting to detect political overtones in the quarrel of the French and Portuguese Knights at Laiazzo. The action very seriously upset the Egyptian plans to build a fleet with which to confront the Portuguese blockade of the spice trade-route in the Red Sea. Spices from the East Indies – pepper, cloves, cinnamon, nutmeg, mace, aloes, ginger, and camphor – were indispensable to the meat-eating Europeans who killed their cattle in autumn and could only store it in brine, or cure or smoke it. Without heavy spicing the stuff was inedible. Since the time of the Pharaohs, for whom spices had a religious significance in the process of embalming, there had been rich rewards from the trade, which was to become the key to the wealth of Constantinople and Venice. It was carried up the Persian Gulf in Muslim ships, thence by camel, and finally in Venetian and Genoese ships to Europe. France had no desire to assist the Portuguese monopoly of this immensely rich trade. If D'Amaral had said something of this sort, L'Isle Adam would not have loved him.

Two sea captains, quarrelling, as all men of fiercely held convictions and different temperaments must sometimes quarrel, about the tactics of a sea fight which is hardly remembered outside the pages of histories of the Order of St. John – a small enough matter it must seem. Yet the consequences of Laiazzo were important. The Muslim confrontation with the Portuguese east of the Red Sea was delayed long enough to allow the 'Lusiads' to reinforce their bases in the Indian Ocean. The brief honeymoon of Ottomans and Mamelukes soon ended. The personal animosity of the two Christian leaders also had repercussions which may have had some influence upon the loss of Rhodes.

· · · · ·

Emeric D'Amboise died on 8th November 1512. The important naval successes of his reign, and the very useful contribution which he made to the consolidation of the Order's position in Europe, tend to be obscured by the long shadow of the great D'Aubusson. His successor was Guy de Blanchefort, nephew of D'Aubusson, Grand Prior of Auvergne, under whose patronage the pretender Djem had lived until his transfer to Rome. He was dying when he embarked at Marseilles for Rhodes; but he knew that he must hurry to the Convent, for the Papacy was again interfering – as the Knights saw it – in the affairs of the Holy Religion; and were the warrior Pope Julius to get wind of Blanchefort's death before the Council in Rhodes, it was feared that he might convene a 'Council' composed of dignitaries created by Rome who would proceed to elect a puppet Grand Master.

Blanchefort's last command was that the great carrack with its galley escort should press on eastwards, and that, as soon as he died, a swift dispatch vessel should be sent ahead to warn the Convent of his death and to urge the Council to elect a successor without delay. He died off Zante, and the news of his death reached Rhodes on 13th October 1513. On the following day, Fabrizio Del Carretto, the Italian hero of St. Nicholas, was elected. He had, in D'Aubusson's prophetic words, 'worried about his future' to good effect. His gallant record and proved capacity for command made him an unexceptionable choice.

Meanwhile, the Ottomans had been having troubles of their own. The relatively peaceable Bajazet had been disposed of, together with his two elder sons, and Selim Yavuz, 'the Grim', was in control. The Ottoman frontier with Persia was too far westward to be safely held, and the Ottoman lands were menaced by a capable and ambitious soldier, Shah Isma'il of the Persian Safavid dynasty, who was also the head of the Shi-ite Dervish Order, with adherents in Anatolia. He was arming for a march westwards – and seeking Christian allies. The war which ensued took on the shape of a struggle for the spiritual leadership of Islam.

Del Carretto saw his opportunity of weakening Selim and allied himself with the Mamelukes, who supported Shah Isma'il and were threatening Selim's southern flank. The alliance was a costly failure. Selim defeated the Shah at Chaldiram in 1514, and then, turning upon the Mamelukes, destroyed their army at Marj Dabik in 1516. In the following year Selim annexed Egypt and claimed to have been invested with the spiritual power of the Caliphate by the last Abbasid puppet of the Circassian Mamelukes. It could not be long before Selim, now Protector of the Faithful, turned his attention to the troublesome island of Rhodes with its arrogant brood of Eblis.

Del Carretto prepared for a siege. Since 1480 there had been much reconstruction and restoration of the defences of Rhodes – as well as of St. Peter, Kos and Lindos, and the other strategic outposts. There was, however, one danger in the near-autonomy of the national Langues: a rich or influential Langue would have the resources to build better defences within the limits of its post. A poor Langue – or one which was having trouble with its national prince or recalcitrant Commanders – tended to neglect its post, and there was not enough pooling of resources. Thus under an Auvergnat Grand Master, the post of Auvergne received special attention (the Boulevard under D'Aubusson); a French Grand Master favoured the post of France (the Gate of D'Amboise); and the Italian Carretto concentrated on the fine complex of new defences at the weak point of 1480, in way of the post of Italy. Nevertheless, Carretto also employed the Emperor Maximilian's personal military engineer, Basilio della Scola di Vicenza, to create a new enceinte in front of the old curtains and towers, which embodied all the latest techniques of angled towers with massive battlements, bastions, ramparts, ravelins and deep ditches with steeply rising escarpments and strongly faced counterscarps, and gun mountings with externally splayed gunports. The Tower of St. Nicholas was also rebuilt with square, steep scarps and mountings for long-range culverins.

Selim was assembling another army – probably against Rhodes – when he died in 1520. Del Carretto, full of years and hard-won honour, followed the Sultan in January 1521, and the stage was now set for the great contest between the seasoned warrior and graceful diplomat, Villiers de L'Isle Adam, and the young Suleiman, only son of the grim Selim.

6

NOTHING SO WELL LOST
1522

Philippe Villiers de L'Isle Adam is a key figure in the history of the Order of the Hospitallers. His fame rests not only upon his defence of Rhodes in 1522; but also upon his faith, courage and tenacity in defeat, without which the end of Rhodes might have spelled – as the Sultan Suleiman meant it to spell – the end of the Holy Religion.

We know what L'Isle Adam looked like in later years. There are engravings and portraits in plenty from his Malta period – including Favray's reconstruction of the ceremonial entry into the capital city of Notabile. He was (in 1530) 'tall, lithe, graceful, alert, with delicate, sensitive face, high cheekbones and aristocratic, aquiline nose, soft, flowing white beard and hair . . . a stern ruler, tactful diplomat and sincere Christian'.[1]

He was born at Beauvais, in the Ile de France, in 1464, a younger son of the great Villiers family, and a kinsman of the Grand Master Jean de Villiers, ruler of the Order at the time of the loss of St. Jean d'Acre in 1291. His family was also connected with the powerful Dukes of Montmorency. Anne de Montmorency, premier Duke and Constable of France, was his nephew, and the Huguenot Admiral Coligny was a cousin.

Villiers joined the Order in his teens and must have reached Rhodes before the ruins of the city and the devastated country-side had been repaired after the attack of 1480. With his family connections it was inevitable that he should become involved in the intrigue which passed for diplomacy, and his later years certainly proved him a diplomat; but he preferred action, and was evidently a competent seaman.

Though his promotion was not as rapid as that of D'Aubusson, Villiers was Seneschal of Rhodes and Captain General of the Galleys (i.e. of the navy) by 1510, at the age of forty-six, and Grand Prior of France before he was fifty. We have already noticed his decisive part in the battle of Laiazzo and his fierce quarrel with D'Amaral about the tactics to be employed.[2]

When the Grand Master Fabrizio Del Carretto died in 1521, L'Isle Adam, now Grand Prior of France, was in Paris. The Order's complex voting system pointed to three candidates for the vacant throne: D'Amaral, now Grand Prior of Castile and Chancellor of the Order; Thomas Docwra, Grand Prior of England, and Turcopilier; and L'Isle Adam.

Carretto had been in failing health during the last year of his reign, and the Chancellor D'Amaral had had virtual control of the Convent and the island. He looked confidently for the succession; but he was arrogant and unpopular, even with his own Langue. Thomas Docwra's candidature was as a 'centre party' man, between the French 'right', and the 'left' of the new Langue of Castile and Leon which had been created expressly to balance the overwhelming French majority in the Order. It is said that at the final count Docwra lost by one vote to L'Isle Adam. D'Amaral was nowhere and, in his chagrin, his fiery temper and unruly tongue drove him to a comment which was to cost him his head.

To his credit, L'Isle Adam had remained in France, making no personal attempt to influence the election. As soon as the result was known the Order's great carrack, the Egyptian *Mogarbina* now christened *Santa Maria*, was dispatched to Marseilles, with an escort of four smaller vessels, to bring the new Grand Master to the Convent. But the Fates seemed to conspire against L'Isle Adam. Off Nice, fire broke out in the brigantine *Reine-des-Mers*, and it was only by threatening to hang any man who deserted that L'Isle Adam was able to bring the fire under control and to save the ship. In a storm in the Malta Channel the *Santa Maria* was struck by lightning. Nine of her company were killed, and the Grand Master's sword was reduced to a cinder – leaving him unscathed: an incident in which pious men were later to see the finger of prophecy. The little flotilla put into Syracuse to repair storm damage. While they lay at anchor, local craft reported that the corsair Cortoglu (Qurd Oghli or Muslih ud-Dhin), now serving under the Ottoman banner, was cruising off the harbour entrance with a powerful galley squadron cleared for action. L'Isle Adam waited until dusk, and fortunate winds and superior seamanship enabled him to evade Cortoglu and to out-distance him during the night.

The Grand Master arrived in Rhodes on 19th September 1521. Suleiman was already riding south flushed with his triumph at Belgrade and bent in his own good time on redressing the failure of his forebear. L'Isle Adam was now fifty-seven – exactly the same age as D'Aubusson had been in 1480.

The Sultan Suleiman II was the great-grandson of Mehmet II, and the only son of Selim the Grim. To Turkish historians who do not recognize Suleiman, son of Bajazet I (1402), Suleiman the Magnificent is known as Suleiman I. It was a blood-stained path which brought him to the imperial throne, and to the Caliphate of Islam, but the blood was not of his shedding. Mehmet's son Bajazet had had three sons. The two elder had inherited their father's essentially peaceable nature; but Selim thirsted for power. He suborned the Janissaries, who had grown restive at Bajazet's inactivity, and with their aid he first deposed and then murdered his father. Having similarly disposed of his two brothers, he proceeded to conquer Syria and then Egypt – making great use of cannon, the 'fire and iron whose use against fellow Muslim was contrary to the spirit and law of Islam'[3] – hanging the Mameluke leader Tuman Bey in 1517.

Selim was preparing a great armada against Rhodes when he died (of 'a cancer')[4] in 1520, and Suleiman – destined to be known in the west as the Magnificent and to his own people as 'Qanuni', the Lawgiver – succeeded without opposition. Suleiman was twenty-six, a poet and a lawyer, a patron of the arts, an outstanding administrator, a religious reformer and a prudent diplomat. A generous and chivalrous foe, his bark with those of his vezirs and pashas who failed him was worse than his bite. Like his contemporary, the English Henry VIII, he resorted to judicial murder as an implement of policy; but rarely of revenge or mere rage. At times his behaviour was a model of courtesy and magnanimity.

L'Isle Adam had scarcely assumed his new responsibilities when Suleiman made his intentions clear.

We may imagine the Grand Master, relaxing for a moment after a month of tiring ceremonies following on his formal reception in the Convent: the Masses and the Te Deums in the

Conventual Church and in the churches of both Latin and Greek rites in the city: the processions and the official presentations of ambassadors, Piliers of the Langues, and the Conventual Bailiffs – all old comrades and shipmates; the two Rhodian bishops, judges, heads of the other religious orders, and distinguished local citizens. And then there had been all the administrative detail, inspections of troops and arms and defences, and the irksome but essential examination of the Treasurer's report.

A cool but correct Chancellor – Andrea D'Amaral – enters to announce the arrival of a messenger from the embassy in Constantinople bearing a letter from the Sultan himself:

> Solyman the sultan, by the grace of God, king of kings, sovereign of sovereigns, most high emperor of Byzantium and Trebizond, very powerful king of Persia, of Arabia, of Syria, and of Egypt, supreme lord of Europe, and of Asia, prince of Mecca and Aleppo, lord of Jerusalem, and ruler of the universal sea, to Philip Villiers de L'Isle Adam, Grand Master of the island of Rhodes, greeting: I congratulate you upon your new dignity, and upon your arrival within your territories. I trust that you will rule there prosperously, and with even more glory than your predecessors. I also mean to cultivate your favour; rejoice then with me, as a very dear friend, that following in the footsteps of my father, who conquered Persia, Jerusalem, Arabia, and Egypt, I have captured that most powerful of fortresses, Belgrade, during the late autumn; after which, having offered battle to the Kuffar, which they had not the courage to accept, I took many other beautiful and well-fortified cities, and destroyed most of their inhabitants either by sword or fire, the remainder being reduced to slavery. Now after sending my numerous and victorious army into their winter quarters, I myself shall return in triumph to my court at Constantinople.

The letter was dated 10th September 1521.

It was not difficult for L'Isle Adam to see the thinly veiled threat. He replied, somewhat more tartly than the niceties of diplomatic correspondence permitted:

> Brother Philip Villiers de L'Isle Adam, Grand Master of Rhodes, to Solyman, sultan of the Turks: I have right well

comprehended the meaning of your letter, which has been presented to me by your ambassador. Your propositions for a peace between us are as pleasing to me as they will be obnoxious to Cortoglu. This pirate during my voyage from France tried to capture me unprepared; in which, when he failed, owing to my having passed into the Rhodian sea by night, he endeavoured to plunder certain merchantmen, that were being navigated by the Venetians; but scarcely had my fleet left their port, than he had to fly, and to abandon the plunder which he had seized from the Cretan merchants. Farewell.[5]

At the same time he wrote to his king, Francis I:

Sire,

De puys la partance du navire qu'a pourté voz [émis?] saires, le Turcq a mandé ici ung sien poste avec ses lectres escriptes à Belgrade le Xe du passé, par lesquelles soubz coulleur d'amytié nous avise qu'il a prins par force le dit Belgrade. . . .

Sire, depuys qu'il est Grand Turcq, ceste-cy est la premiere lectre qu'il a envoyé a Rhodes, laquelle n'acceptons pour signiffiance d'amytié, mais plutôt pour une menasse couverte. . . .[6]

Since the departure of the vessel which brought your emissaries[?], the Turk has sent letters written at Belgrade on the 10th of last month, in which under the colour of friendship he informs us that he has taken that city by force. . . .

Sire, since he became Grand Turk, this is the first letter that he has sent to Rhodes, and we do not accept it as a token of friendship; but rather as a veiled threat. . . .

This letter was dated 28th October 1521.

Other letters followed, and there was talk of 'tribute'; but it was clear that, tribute or none, Suleiman was determined sooner or later to liquidate the Hospitallers. On 10th June 1522 – by which time Suleiman's armada had already assembled at Constantinople and an advance squadron was attacking Kos – L'Isle Adam received the Sultan's ultimatum:

The Sultan Solyman to Villiers de L'Isle Adam, Grand Master of Rhodes, to his Knights, and to the people at large. Your monstrous injuries against my most afflicted people

have aroused my pity and indignation. I command you, therefore, instantly to surrender the island and fortress of Rhodes,
and I give you my gracious permission to depart in safety with
the most precious of your effects; or if you desire to remain
under my government, I shall not require of you any tribute,
or do aught in diminution of your liberties, or against your
religion. If you are wise, you will prefer friendship and peace
to a cruel war. Since, if you are conquered, you will have to
undergo all such miseries as are usually inflicted by those that
are victorious, from which you will be protected neither by
your own forces, nor by external aid, nor by the strength of
your fortifications which I will overthrow to their foundations.
If, therefore, you prefer my friendship to war, there shall be
neither fraud nor stratagem used against you. I swear this by
the God of heaven, the Creator of the earth, by the four
Evangelists, by the four thousand Prophets, who have descended from heaven, chief amongst whom stands Mahomet,
most worthy to be worshipped; by the shades of my grandfather and father, and by my own sacred, august, and imperial
head.

No reply was sent.
Turkish writers are quite clear about the justification for
Suleiman's descent on Rhodes. Mustafa Gelal-Zade wrote:[7]

It was the determination of the Padishah, Father of the
World and Conqueror of the Earth, to move against Buda,
capital of the unhappy land of Hungary; but one sect of the
accursed 'Firenghi', worst of the sons of error, sent by Sheitan
and noted for cunning and artifice, outcasts, accursed workers
of iniquity, expert seamen and outstanding navigators, possessed great fortresses in all parts of the Mediterranean coast.
In the straits and upon the islands inhabited by these obstinate
vipers there were wide lands and strong forts in mountain and
plain. These infidels were masters of much territory . . . and
their Corsairs, noted for their energy and courage, attacked
and cut the sea routes, causing great loss and suffering to peace-
ful merchants, capturing or destroying their ships and carrying
the people off into slavery. Above all, the fortified city of
Rhodes was a refuge for these accursed Franks. Its fortresses

were without equal and its defences incomparable in all the earth, and here these souls destined for Eblis had their secure refuge whence they sent out their swift galleys to the hurt and loss of Islam, permitting no merchant or pilgrim ship to pass towards Egypt unharmed by their cannon, enslaving and putting chains upon the free and the innocent. . . . How many children of the Prophet fall prisoner to the people of error? How many have chains put about their necks and gyves upon their ankles? How many thousands of the Faithful are forced to deny their Faith? How many virgins and young women? How many wives and infants? . . . Their malignity knows no end. . . . The Sultans of the Jihad thought their conquest impossible . . . Mehmet Khan, now eternally in Paradise, may God illumine his tomb, sent the Grand Vezir Misac Pasha with valorous men . . . but they returned disconsolate. From that time [Rhodes] has increased in strength and confidence. It is the outpost of all the Infidel lands from whence come sustenance and treasure. The pride and the persistence in error of those evil men have closed and barred all the sea routes. Therefore, the Padishah, whose strength is of the Angels, the protected of God, the companion of Khidr, inspired and favoured by God . . . saw fit to conquer Rhodes. . . . Once more the shout is raised whose echo fills the earth. The Lord of Time goes to war. Old and young raise your hands in prayer. Rejoice, for all is prepared. . . .

The Grand Master could hope for little help from princes or Papacy. France and Spain were still locked in their struggle and still using Italy as a battlefield. Charles V, son of the poor, mad Spanish Queen Joanna and the handsome Philip of Flanders, had succeeded to the Empire, which now embraced Spain, the Netherlands and a nominal overlordship of Germany; but the German-Swiss Reformation was in full flood and the shrunken German 'Reich' left by the Emperor Maximilian I was as disordered and frustrated as ever. Eastern Europe was in no shape to face a determined Ottoman attack. Poland survived; but still in fear of the Muscovites and their implacable hatred of the Latin Church, their determination to found a new Byzantium and to conquer 'the patrimony of St. Vladimir'.

England had recovered much of her power; but Henry VIII was already threatening the properties of the Hospitallers, hoping that the proceeds would help pay for his costly and pointless little wars in France.

Pope Leo X (Giovanni de Medici) had momentarily halted the disruptive movement in the Church in France; but he was as Luther called him 'a lamb amongst lions'. The Dominican Tetzel's exaggerated interpretation of Leo's famous Indulgence, intended to raise funds for the Basilica of St. Peter, had merely hastened the destruction of Christian unity.

The Dutchman Adrian Florenz – tutor to the Emperor Charles V – who succeeded Leo as Adrian VI (1522–23), did his scholarly best; but his epitaph in the German church of Santa Maria dell' Anima in Rome might well stand as the epitaph of the age: 'Alas, even with the best of men, how much depends on the times in which he lives.'

Throughout the winter and spring of 1521–22 the spies were busy. The Sultan Selim had planted a Jewish doctor in the heart of the Convent, in the Hospital. He was ostensibly a Christian convert and was to remain undetected until the autumn of 1522, by which time the siege was well advanced. He sent his messages by the hand of merchants who passed to and from Rhodes by way of Turkish-occupied Chios. Early in 1522 he reported that the Boulevard of Auvergne was again under reconstruction, that some of the Italian Knights were mutinous and wished to return to their Commanderies where the Pope was once more disposing of benefices, and that there was a powerful faction in favour of coming to terms with Suleiman.

L'Isle Adam's spies had little difficulty in reporting to St. Peter on the mainland, whence their reports were transmitted by fast dispatch vessels. He learned from them that Suleiman was assembling an armada and enrolling troops from all over his empire. Mustafa Pasha, his brother-in-law, had been appointed Commander-in-Chief, and the corsair Cortoglu had been engaged as naval chief-of-staff. All Turkish ports were closed, and arrivals were at once chartered or expropriated. It was also said that Suleiman had not been enthusiastic about a descent on Rhodes at this particular moment; but Mustafa had persuaded him – aided by the agents' reports about the state of the garrison. Rossi quotes an anonymous Turkish MS. which says that Suleiman was finally convinced when his dead mother appeared to him in a dream and assured him of victory. He also notes a single Turkish reference to a threatened insurrection inspired by the merchants of Constantinople who desired the liquidation of the corsairs of Rhodes.

The Grand Master pressed on with his preparations to receive Suleiman. The new bastion of Auvergne was hurried forward. All the ditches were deepened and widened. Victuals and munitions were ordered from Naples and the Romagna, and wine – a medical necessity of the times – from Candia. The Servant-at-Arms Antonio Bosio, kinsman of the historian and evidently a skilled negotiator, was able to extract fifteen ship-loads of Cretan wine from the reluctant Venetians and to enroll soldiers under the guise of wine-porters. Not all Venetians were neutral. One, Master Bonaldi, bound for Constantinople with a cargo of 700 casks of wine, voluntarily put into Rhodes and offered his services to the Order. A Genoese, Domenico Fornari, bound from Alexandria for Constantinople with grain, was less warlike than Bonaldi. Ordered to heave-to by a patrolling galley, eight miles from Rhodes, he protested that his first duty was to his owners and charterers and the cargo owners. He was 'persuaded' – and later did good service.

The Order's navy was sent far and wide amongst the islands to bring in all but small holding forces from the outposts. Two galleys were kept on patrol in the waters of the Gulf of Kos with orders to send back sighting reports at the first sign of Suleiman's armada.

By the end of April everything harvestable had been brought into the city. The pleasant gardens and villas in the approaches to the city had been scorched.

In May L'Isle Adam staged a general review of the Langues, the citizen militia and foreign mercenaries. He seems to have cheated a little, marching some units past twice to put heart into the people. The two bishops – the Latin, Genoese Leonardo Balestrieri, and the Greek Clement – both men of high reputation, were enjoined to preach encouraging sermons and to prepare the Rhodians for the coming Holy War.

The garrison was organized so as to leave no crossing channels of command, while still allowing room for flexibility and initiative. Four Grand Crosses commanded a mobile reserve, by sectors: D'Amaral for Auvergne and Germany; the English Turcopilier, John Buck, for Aragon and England; the French Grand Prior, Pierre de Cluys, for France and Castile; and the Prior of Navarre, Gregoire de Morgut, for Provence and Italy. Fra Didier de Tholon, Bailiff of Manosque, was in overall command of artillery.

The city was put under martial law and a tribunal of four Grand Crosses was appointed with powers of life and death. They were Claude de St. Prie and Jean Boniface of France, Inigo Lope de Ayala and Ugo Capones of Aragon. The key Tower of St. Nicholas was commanded by the Provençal Guidot de Castellac. Each national post was under separate command: Fra Raimond Ricard at Provence, Jean de St. Simon at France, Raimond Rogier at Auvergne, Giorgio Aimari at Italy, William Weston at England. Juan de Barbaran at Aragon, Christopher Waldners at Germany and Fernando de Sollier at Castile and Portugal.

The palace of the Grand Master (whose northern wall was an integral part of the post of France) was entrusted to the Englishman Thomas Sheffield, Commander of Beverley and Seneschal of the Grand Master.

Each of the five major bastions had its commander: Jean de Mesnyl for Auvergne, Tomas Escarrieros for Spain, Nicholas Hussey for England, Jean de Brinquier de Lioncel for Provence and Andreotto Gentile for Italy. The Grand Master's standard was entrusted to Henry Mansell of England.

The commercial port was closed with two great chains backed up by booms, and the galley port was blocked, except for a single narrow channel, by sunken hulks full of stones.

Legates were dispatched to the new Pope – the Dutchman Adrian VI, from whom much was hoped – to the Emperor Charles V, to Francis I and Henry VIII; but there was little to be expected beyond the usual promises. Pantaleone says that 'they were all distracted by their wars in Flanders and Italy'; that Cardinal Giulio de Medici (later Pope Clement VII), himself a member of the Order of St. John, pressed the Pope to send a force to the relief of Rhodes, but that Adrian VI preferred to use it against the French.

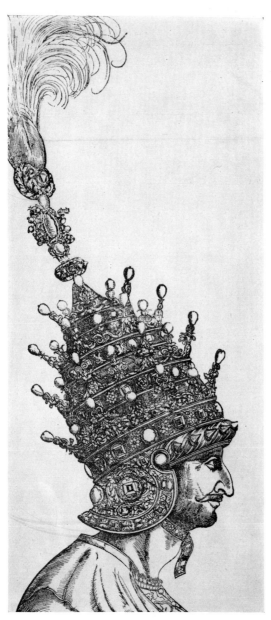

Suleiman the magnificent, from
an engraving by Agostino Veneziano

A Knight of Rhodes, from a painting by Pinturicchio

Three Commissioners were charged with the control of victuals, weapons and ammunition, and by the end of May they were able to report that the fortress was capable of holding out for a year. They were Andrea D'Amaral, the Chancellor, Fra Gabriel de Pommerols, the Grand Commander and Lieutenant of the Grand Master, and John Buck, the Turcopilier.

Suleiman's Grand Vezir in 1522 was Pir Mehmed (or Peri Mahmud) Pasha, acclaimed by the Turkish poets as a direct descendant of the great Abu Bakr, the Companion of the Prophet – and, if this was true, an Arab. The second Vezir was Mustafa Pasha – later to be relieved of his post by the Sultan and 'kicked upstairs' to govern Egypt. Vertot gives him every credit for personal bravery.[8] He was a brother-in-law of the Sultan and an experienced soldier, though of advancing years. The third Vezir, who took over Mustafa's command, was Ahmed Pasha, an Albanian who had been promoted to Beylerbey of Rumelia after the siege of Belgrade. Turkish historians describe him as a man of 'bad character, envious and proud; ambitious for the post of Grand Vezir. After the conquest of Rhodes he asked for and obtained the governorship of Egypt, where he rebelled in 1524; being slain and his head carried to Constantinople. . . .'[9]

Amongst the subordinate commanders was Ayas Pasha, another Albanian, who had been Agha of the Janissaries and was to follow Ahmed as Beylerbey of Rumelia. He incurred the Sultan's displeasure at Rhodes and was placed under arrest. Pardoned, he became Grand Vezir in 1537. According to the Turkish records he was a 'prudent and just man'.[10]

The Agha of the Janissaries was Bali Agha – seriously wounded in the assault. The poets describe him as 'like a raging lion'. Qasim Pasha, who commanded the forces before the post of England, was a son of a slave of the Sultan Bajazet II – 'first in the ranks of the heroes of Anatolia'.[11] The Admiral was Pilaq Mustafa Pasha, but his chief-of-staff, the corsair Cortoglu, was virtually in command of the Ottoman fighting fleet.

Before assembling the expeditionary force for Rhodes, Suleiman had sent Ferhad Pasha to Shiwas (or Siwas) to deal with a rebellion by the Shi-ite Shah-Suwar Oghli Ali Bey. By 5th June 1522 the Turkish accounts say that he had gathered 700 ships in Constantinople, with 40,000 seamen and 20,000 Azab or irregulars. The second Vezir Mustafa Pasha was in command of the fleet which sailed for Gallipoli (in the Dardanelles), where they were joined by Pilaq Mustafa, the Qapudan of Gallipoli, with more ships and by Cortoglu. Thence they sailed for Chios, leaving that island, some for Rhodes and some for Marmarice, on 16th June.

Meanwhile, Suleiman himself was marching via Scutari, Mal Tepe and Yeni Sheher towards Kutahia, where he was joined on 1st July by the Beylerbey of Anatolia, Qasim Pasha, the Agha of the Janissaries, Bali Pasha, and the Agha of the Azab, Ali Bey. On 2nd July Ayas Pasha arrived there with his forces; and on 11th July Ferhad Pasha met the Sultan on the march with the severed heads of the rebel Shah-Suwar and his three sons. On 26th July Suleiman, now some days behind the body of the army, arrived at Marmarice.

While Suleiman marched south, his ultimatum had reached Rhodes in a very curious manner. On the night of 8th June signal flares had been seen in the direction of Physcos; and a brigantine commanded by the Frenchman Fra Mennetou, with a purser of the fleet, one Jacob Jaxi, who spoke Turkish, was sent to investigate. An exchange of hostages was proposed and Jaxi was sent ashore. He did not return and later reports had it that he had been taken to Suleiman and tortured into betraying all he knew about the Order's preparations. A galley was sent to support Mennetou and the vessels returned bearing Suleiman's letter (quoted on p. 115).

Messages from Kos now reported an advance force of thirty sail, landing Sipahis and seizing peasants and fishermen. When the Sipahis approached the fortress they were set upon by the Bailiff, Prejan de Bidoux, few escaping alive. The Bailiff had his horse shot under him.

These early encounters were probably intended mainly to collect prisoners and to test the strength of the enemy. A raid by Fra Jean Beauluoys (nicknamed 'the Wolf') captured a Turkish brig whose crew insisted that the main fleet consisted of no more than 200 sail, badly armed, old and cranky. There were Christian slaves in all the galleys. The Janissaries were opposed to the expedition, and it was hoped to overcome Rhodes by mining; hence Suleiman had collected a force of expert sappers from his Bosnian and Wallachian territories.

If L'Isle Adam needed confirmation about likely Turkish tactics, he now had it. He at once sent to Candia, asking for the services of an engineer and mining expert, Gabriele Tadini da Martinengo, now in the service of Venice.

Among the many able men whom L'Isle Adam attracted to his side in 1522 Tadini was perhaps the most outstanding. A Bergamese soldier and military engineer,[12] Gabriele Tadino, commonly known as Gabriele Tadini da Martinengo, was called by Bosio 'Il Bresciano', and his family did originate in Brescia. Only Bosio calls Tadini a Brescian. Promis points out that Brescia, Bergamo and Cremona have all claimed the great artillerist and engineer as their son; but Gabriele was born, some time in 1480, the second of three sons of Clemente Tadino, at the great castle of Martinengo, twelve miles from the city of Bergamo. Martinengo had been acquired by his grandfather Michele, a Brescian who had somehow amassed a fortune and great possessions in Bergamo and Cremona. Originally intended for the profession of medicine, the young Gabriele's imagination was captured by the new arts of war – of military architecture, and of the possibilities of gunpowder. In Bergamo, he studied under a French military engineer, whose name has apparently not survived, and was twenty-nine before he entered the service of the Venetian republic in 1509. He must already have earned some reputation, for he was immediately commissioned as a 'Captain of Infantry with the rank of Engineer'.[13] He fought against the French at Padua and was wounded and taken prisoner at Brescia in 1512. Released at the conclusion of peace with France, Gabriele was kept busy restoring the war-damaged fortifications throughout the recovered Venetian territories and was promoted to 'Engineer General and Colonel of Infantry'.[14] In 1516 he was fighting the Spaniards at Bergamo. They, in their turn, being expelled from the Venetian republic, Gabriele was sent to Crete, where he was given supreme command of artillery and charged with strengthening the defence against a probable Turkish war. His clandestine flight from Crete to Rhodes in 1522, at the instigation of Antonio Bosio, was the beginning of a long association with the Hospitallers, to whom he was to render excellent service.[15] Gallizioli, who wrote his biography, says that L'Isle Adam was so concerned that the Turks would try, in spite of the terms of the capitulation of 1522, to possess themselves of so valuable a man that he smuggled Gabriele out of Rhodes at night.

We know what this splendid soldier looked like from a rare – and almost certainly contemporary – portrait in the Galleria Tadini at Lovere, probably painted between 1538 and 1543. He shows us only the undamaged side of a strong, clever face with grim, determined mouth, a great prow of a nose and the creases of laughter around his single eye. He is clothed in the habit of a Knight of Rhodes and is wearing the bronze medal which was struck in his honour in 1538, showing the obverse, which displays a battery of cannon and the date MCCCCCXXXVIII, with the inscription 'Ubi ratio ibi fortuna'. On the reverse is a relief of his own profile.[16]

Venice was neutral in 1522 – 'Veneziani poi Cristiani' – and the Governor of Candia, the Duke of Trevisani, 'feared the Signoria more than he feared the Turks'.[17] When he heard of the Grand Master's invitation, he forbade Tadini to leave Crete, and threatened dire penalties for assisting his escape. This was a task for the astute Antonio Bosio.

Through his 'grapevine' in Candia, Bosio arranged a rendezvous in a remote part of the Bay of Mirabella eastward of Candia. Tadini, a typical Lombard, a ferocious partisan of causes, combining virtuosity with flamboyance and physical bravery, did not hesitate. But his escape was soon reported, and as his horse galloped across the sand, the guard ship from Candia was sighted entering the bay in full chase. Bosio unstepped his masts and spread his brown sails, covering his vessel from stem to stern and from bulwark to waterline. He then warped himself in under a cliff with grapnels – and became invisible. Nightfall and a strong westerly breeze enabled Bosio and Tadini, with his friends Conversalo and Scaramosa, to slip away and to reach Rhodes some days after the arrival of the Turkish advance force of thirty sail, which had been sighted on 25th June when fifteen miles distant from Kum Burnu.

The Turks had sailed past the city, within cannon shot, with colours flying and bands playing; a gesture of defiance which was met by a broadside from Fort St. Nicholas – name of ill omen to any Turk who remembered 1480.

On 26th June, the Feast of Corpus Domini, which was celebrated as usual in the city,[18] the advance squadron anchored some six miles to the south of Rhodes in Kalitheas Bay, behind Cape Voudhi; and for the next fourteen days convoys of transports and auxiliary craft were arriving from Physcos. Sansovino says the Turkish fleet originally anchored off Villa Nuova on the northwest coast, and that after they moved to 'Capo di Bove' (Voudhi) they came under fire from a huge cannon mounted near the gate of St. John, which 'soon burst'. If such a cannon existed it would need to have had a range of three and a half miles.[19]

Bourbon puts the total force in Kalitheas Bay at 103 galleys, thirty-five galeasses, fifteen mahons and twenty smaller craft. These were to be joined later by a fleet from Syria, bringing the total, distributed between Rhodes and Marmarice, to 400 sail, bearing an army of 200,000 men with all their gear, of whom 60,000 were skilled miners. All these figures are inflated; but by contemporary standards it was a formidable force.

To confront this force it is estimated that the Holy Religion could muster 500 Knights and Servants-at-Arms, 1,000 mercenary soldiers and perhaps 500 Rhodian militia. In 1513, a year of relative peace, some 600 votes had been cast in the election of Del Carretto, but this total included Chaplains as well as Knights and Servants-at-Arms. (In 1476, 350 voted at the election of D'Aubusson.) Reinforcements, totalling perhaps fifty Knights and gentlemen adventurers and one or two hundred soldiers and sailors reached the city during the siege.

No disembarkation was started by the Ottomans until the whole armada had assembled. A bold proposal submitted by a Florentine ship's captain, one Bartoluzzi, was seriously considered, but at length discarded on grounds of its cost in vessels, combustibles and explosives. Bartoluzzi wanted to equip a fleet of fireships (there was adequate shipping in the port), and send them down amongst the Turks at night before landings started. If surprise could have been achieved, there is no doubt that crippling damage to the invaders was likely. But L'Isle Adam seems sometimes to have been overcautious. He preferred to keep his ships intact, and his powder and his pitch for a more certain purpose.

By the second week in July [20] disembarkation started – heavy cannon, with their ponderous carriages, powder and stone and brass shot, timber, cordage, picks and shovels, ox-hides, rams, bores, stakes, draught animals (for the Rhodians had left no animals in their farms or fields), grain, dried and salted mutton and goat, cooking pots, tents, luxurious pavilions for the Pashas – and all the gear and the men with their armour and their weapons had to travel over rough hilly ground as far as the road which led from Koskino to the city.

The first Turkish battery was installed on the hillside known from a church of that name as Saints Cosmas and Damian, facing the post of England; and fire was opened while the pioneers hurried on the erection of palisades. The second battery faced the post of Provence and the third the tower of Spain, in the post of Aragon. The first results were discouraging for the besiegers. A furious return-fire from the city wrecked the batteries and chased the wretched pioneers beyond cannon shot.

The Turks had been harassed by sorties throughout their disembarkation, and the sorties continued to cut off small bodies and working parties until the losses had run into scores. Christian sources talk of a mutiny which was not quelled until the arrival of the Sultan. Turkish sources make no such mention, but there does seem to have been an early difference of opinion about the use of artillery, Pir Mehmed Pasha contending that it was a waste of shot to fire into the city or, at this early stage, to use any but the heaviest bombards against the defences.[21]

On 28th July – the fourth day of Ramadan – Suleiman arrived from Physcos with a further battalion of Janissaries, and landed to the firing of salutes and the bellicose music of the Janissaries' band. He made his way to a villa at Megasandra, a village four or five miles to the south-west of the city, where he established his headquarters.

The besieging forces were now disposed in a nearly symmetrical crescent, enclosing the enceinte. Pir Mehmed Pasha, the Grand Vezir and descendant of Abu Bakr, was close to the sea with his right flank on the Bay of Acandia, facing the post of Italy: Mustafa Pasha, the second Vezir, was on Pir Mehmed's left, facing Provence, with Qasim Pasha, the Beylerbey of Anatolia, on his left, facing England. Ahmed Pasha faced the tower of Spain (Aragon), with Ayas Pasha on his left, before Auvergne. Bali, the Agha of the Janissaries, stood before Germany and the post of France, with his left flank towards the galley port – but not too close to the sea, because of the powerful batteries of St. Nicholas.

The corsair Cortoglu commanded the fighting galleys and the armed carracks. His task was to ensure a blockade of the two harbours, and to bombard the city and the commercial port as opportunity offered.

On 9th August more ships, with a number of small craft and a force of Janissaries and Mamelukes sent by Khair Bey, arrived from Syria, and the fresh troops were allocated to Pir Pasha's sector.

Accounts of the disposition and calibre of the Ottoman artillery vary. Bourbon reckons that sixty to eighty major pieces were originally sited in batteries of three or four; but that the counter-bombardment of the Knights soon reduced these by half. Thereafter, he says, there were never less than thirty-four large cannon serviceable at any moment. He itemizes twelve bombards firing balls of nine to eleven palms (seven to nine feet) in circumference, twelve basilisks with six-foot balls, fifteen iron and bronze cannon with four- to five-foot balls, six bronze cannon with three-foot balls. There were also fifteen double cannon firing iron balls, twelve bronze mortars firing six-foot balls, plus an incredible number of smaller pieces for firing small *carcasses* and other fancy projectiles. Four of the heaviest pieces were at once mounted opposite the bastions of England and Aragon, and two opposite Italy. The mortars were distributed: eight against England, and firing into the Jews' Quarter; two in front of the Koskino (or St. John's) Gate; and two in front of Auvergne.

Bourbon's own count of the Turkish projectiles fired from 29th July to the end of August gives 1,316 stone balls and eight of the largest *carcasses*; but he adds that 'others say 1,721, and others 2,000'. Little was achieved by firing into the city. In one month of continuous bombardment there were no more than twenty-five killed.

·　　·　　·　　·　　·

On 29th July the siege opened in earnest. Under cover of a furious bombardment, the Turks commenced digging trenches and carting stones and earth for a vast earthwork in Ahmed's sector, facing the tower of Aragon. The loss of life amongst the miserable Azab was serious, and work on the earthwork was suspended until nightfall. The purpose of the work was not at once apparent to the defenders, and a Rhodian called Basil (or Basilios) Carpazio[22] volunteered to find his way with a picked body of companions, all of whom spoke Turkish, into the Turkish lines.

Basil rowed stealthily out of the galley port at night in a fishing craft. At a safe distance he hoisted his sail and made towards the Gulf of Symi. In the morning he went about and sailed back – with a catch of fish – to the beach at Acandia behind Pir Mehmet's lines, where something resembling a market had been set up by the Turkish camp-followers. It was not difficult for Basil and his crew to mingle with the crowd of Turks, Circassians, Arabs, Anatolians, Persians and arrogant Janissaries off duty, and little more difficult to entice two or three idling soldiers into the boat at dusk. In the course of knocking them on the head, one proved so difficult that Basil was forced to decapitate him; but that evening he was able to report to the Grand Master with one Turkish head and two thoroughly scared prisoners. From them it was learned that the purpose of the earthwork was to erect a battery above the level of the battlements, in the hope of silencing the guns of the defence while the all-important work of completing the entrenchments and commencing the undermining of the walls went forward.

On 1st August, exercising his prerogative, the Grand Master received Gabriele Tadini da Martinengo as a Knight of Magistral Grace in the Langue of Italy, investing him with the Grand Cross and granting him the right of succession to the first vacant bailiwick in the Italian Langue. Tadini had already commenced his countermining operations, and slaves were busy tunnelling under the walls and bastions, while picked teams of Rhodians were being trained in the use of Tadini's 'mine detectors' – parchment stretched on drums with little bells attached which signalled every impact of an enemy pick.

On 1st August, also, the Turks opened fire on the post of

Germany and kept it up for ten days, their fire being returned round for round by the German gunners until the attackers were at last compelled to abandon their batteries – though not before they had destroyed the prominent tower of the church of St. John, a valuable observation post, whose bells had also been useful for a system of calls and alarms.

Twelve batteries were then shifted, in the night, to the foreshore opposite the Tower of St. Nicholas; but their incessant pounding was totally ineffectual. The Florentine engineers had made an excellent job of reconstructing the tower, and the gunnery of the garrison was so good that the Turks could not man their guns for longer than an hour a day at each battery. They then tried night bombardment, but were no more successful, finally shifting the batteries to reinforce the attack on the posts of England and Aragon where, in Ahmed's sector, the enemy earthwork overtopped the battlements by ten to twelve feet. There were now fourteen batteries – virtually the whole of the heavy artillery – concentrated in Ahmed's sector, and by 14th August the Turks had succeeded in battering down a great part of the new ravelins and ramparts, as well as damaging the bastion of England. The older wall, or curtain, stood up better than was expected. But soon there was a clear breach in the curtain of Aragon, and the fallen masonry had filled the ditch, and it was not long before there were open breaches in the walls of England and Provence. The damage was repaired overnight; but by day the cannonade re-opened the walls, and the plunging fire from the batteries on the earthwork was causing heavy casualties. The English, in particular, had suffered in the sorties as well as from the bombardment, and some of the mobile reserve had to be sent to reinforce them in anticipation of an expected assault.

In the artillery duel, the Turkish master gunner Mehmed, the son of the famous artillerist Topgi Basha, had lost both legs, and Rostam, the Spanish master gunner, had been killed. Suleiman remarked of Mehmed that he 'would rather it had happened to any of his Pashas'.[23]

There had been heavy casualties, too, at the post of Aragon. Juan de Barbaran, the Commander, had been killed, and Juan D'Homedes (who was to succeed L'Isle Adam as Grand Master of Malta in 1536) had lost an eye.

On 14th August a shot from a mortar in Pir Pasha's sector landed on the aftercastle of a Genoese carrack in the commercial port, sinking her. By 19th August there was a breach in the curtain of Italy and the Turkish trenches had reached the counterscarp. The sappers were burrowing into the fallen masonry and making a covered way under the ravelin and right up to the ramparts.

Tadini needed time to build retrenchments and to complete his own tunnelling. L'Isle Adam, who had moved his headquarters to the church of Our Lady of Victories, was persuaded to approve a series of sorties – though he could ill afford any casualties. On the 19th there was a sortie in Pir Pasha's sector, Tadini himself leading 200 mounted Knights and men-at-arms up to Pir's cannon, spitting the men in the trenches on their pikes as they rode, setting fire to the batteries, and drawing off reinforcements from beneath the walls. As they retired, Bourbon says, the Turks coming after them 'through the gardens' suffered heavily from musket fire. There were similar sorties and hard fighting in Pir Pasha's sector on the 20th, and in Ahmed's and Ayas Pasha's sectors on the 22nd and 24th, the Knights returning with live prisoners, and turbanned heads on their pikes.

There was an unhappy incident on 23rd August when a party of slaves, returning to their quarters from working on the ramparts of Auvergne, were 'buffeted in play' by some badly behaved young Knights. The slaves retaliated, and the guards on duty, thinking that the enemy had broken in, opened fire, killing twenty slaves. Bourbon regrets the incident because 'the slaves were innocent and their loss deprived us of not a few able sappers'.

On 24th August Fra Emeric Depreaux, who had been sent to Europe to seek aid, returned with a cargo of victuals, a handful of soldiers, three or four Knights and the usual promises.

There were now so many breaches that a general assault could not long be delayed. The indefatigable Antonio Bosio was sent off to Naples and Rome, and Fra Nicholas Hussey to Provence, to try once more for something more solid than promises. They sailed together on 28th August. The ease with which ships had come and gone says nothing for the efficiency of Cortoglu's blockade. Perhaps there was something in the report that Suleiman's fleet consisted of old and cranky vessels. Perhaps it was not

Cortoglu's kind of war. Eventually Suleiman lost his temper with the renowned 're'is', and he suffered the supreme indignity of being bastinadoed on the quarter deck of his own flagship.

Tadini was now making traverses on the walls on either side of all the breaches, and mounting mixed batteries of heavy cannon and man-killing weapons covering the approach trenches and the breaches themselves. Marksmen with the new quick-aiming muskets were posted on strategic roofs and towers. As the enemy emerged like moles from their covered ways, under the shattered ramparts, they were mowed down by the score; but still they came on until they were sheltering under the bastions beneath pent-houses of raw hides – still tunnelling and boring away at the masonry.

On 2nd September the Sultan learned that the 're'is' Qara Mahmud, who had been sent to occupy Tilos, had been killed, but that the island had surrendered.

The bombardment went on – ever widening the existing gaps in the walls, and wrecking more and more of the dwellings in the town. Pantaleone reports the use of a particularly nasty projectile in the form of a *carcasse* bound with an integument of cord which gave off a 'nauseous stink' and which was studded with tiny slivers of metal. A wound from one of these immediately turned septic – clearly a refinement of the commoner forms of bacteriological war.

By early September it was estimated that five-sixths of the enceinte had been undermined with tunnels, of which there were at least fifty running in different directions; but Tadini had rendered most of them abortive. He had cut continuous subways from the Gate of D'Amboise to the tower of Aragon, and from the bastion of England to the Koskino Gate, thence to the bastion of Del Carretto in the post of Italy. Tadini's tunnels ran across the direction of those of the Turks, confronting them at every point.

The first Turkish mine was detected under the wall of Provence. Tadini's listening post reported and he set off a counter-mine. The miserable miners who were not burned or suffocated fled.

On the afternoon of 4th September, a mine detonated under the bastion of England caused the whole city to quake and made a gap thirty-six feet wide in the face of the bastion. The Turks rushed from their trenches on to the already shattered ramparts and gained a foothold on the bastion itself, planting banners on the wall. The English met them with swords and pikes, and the musketeers, arquebusiers and archers fired into the press of the advancing assailants. The great Bergamese, Tadini, was there with the Captain of the Galleys, Michel D'Argillemont, who was struck in the eye by an arrow. The Grand Master himself, with Henry Mansell bearing the banner of the Crucifixion presented to D'Aubusson in 1480, hurried from Benediction in the church of Our Lady of Victories to help the hard-pressed English. The slaughter was too much for the Turks who began to fall back. Mustafa himself was with the first wave of the attack; but he was borne back into the ditch by the weight of the fugitives. He laid about him with his scimitar, and by means of insults, encourage-ments and threats compelled a fresh assault. The hand-to-hand fighting lasted two hours. The Ottomans retired to their trenches and behind their palisades, leaving many dead and wounded (who were not spared) in the rubble and on the parapets. Fra D'Argille-mont, the Captain of the Galleys, was to die of wounds, as were the Grand Commander Gabriel de Pommerols and the standard bearer, Henry Mansell.

On 6th September Suleiman was cheered by the appearance of the elders of Nisyros, bearing the keys of their city in voluntary surrender to Islam.[24]

On 9th September two mines were set off under Provence – ineffectually, thanks to Tadini. Another beneath the English bastion was partly effective, destroying another six feet of masonry. The attackers, who were waiting in the trenches for the explosion before advancing, fled when the new standard bearer, Fra Joachim de Cluys of the French Langue, appeared on the ramparts with the Grand Master's banner. The guns on the towers of Koskino (St. John's Gate) wrecked a section of trench, killing and burying the occupants; but Mustafa once more flogged and shamed his men into returning to the breach. More bloody hand-to-hand work followed and a Turkish standard was captured. Bourbon apologizes for there being no more enemy standards, but he explains that it was now difficult to pursue the retreating enemy because Mustafa had cut 'fox-holes' all along the counter-scarp of the ditch and manned them with sharpshooters. Turkish losses were optimistically estimated at 2–3,000. Bourbon admits to thirty Christian men-at-arms killed and many more wounded. Fra Guyot de Marsillac, the local Commander of Artillery, was badly wounded and Joachim de Cluys lost an eye.

Very similar assaults followed on the 11th against England, with heavy losses to both sides, and on the 13th and 14th all along the front of Ahmed's and Mustafa's sectors, accompanied by feverish mining and countermining as a prelude to each assault. On 18th September Ahmed lost some hundreds of men – many of them the victims of his own mines or of the counter-mining efforts of Tadini.[25] Losses were heavy amongst the garrison, too. The Prior of St. Gilles, of the Provençal Langue, the redoubtable Prejan de Bidoux, had his throat cut 'from side to side', but recovered.

On 19th September[26] the treachery of the Jewish doctor, whom Fontanus calls Apella Renato, was discovered. He was incautious enough to allow himself to be caught in the act of shooting a bolt from a crossbow charged with a message for Pir Pasha, in which he reported that the garrison was reduced to extremes. Under the question he confessed to having been in communication with the Ottomans since the time of Selim, and to having fired five previous messages into the enemy camp since the siege commenced. He had, amongst other advice, warned that mortar fire into the city was a waste of powder and shot. Bourbon says that after being condemned to hanging and quartering the Jew confessed his sins and 'died a good Christian'.

On the 20th there was a fierce assault in Pir Pasha's sector on the badly damaged post of Italy, followed very shortly by simultaneous assaults on Provence, England and Aragon. The Turks occupied the remains of the tower and the bastion of Aragon and claim to have captured five Christian banners.[27] After some hours of merciless slaughter in which the Knights used every imaginable weapon – swords, pikes, muskets and crossbows, Greek fire, boiling pitch and oil, stones and, as the enemy eventually made off in disorder, small cannon or 'murthering pieces' – the bastion was regained. Bosio says that the Christian casualties were 200; but that the Turks lost 20,000.[28] We may be content with a ten to one ratio.

On 22nd September a mine under the post of Aragon was

harmlessly 'ventilated' by Tadini; but a second, under Auvergne, shook the city and destroyed the whole of the internal (or older) wall. However, the new masonry was undamaged because Tadini had bored a series of 'spiral vents' through which the blast was dispersed. Turkish reports say that one of these explosions killed a number of Janissaries who had not retired in time.

From sunset on 23rd September the look-outs reported great activity in the Turkish lines. Bodies of men could be heard moving in the gardens, away from the northern flank of the besieging crescent, and by first light it was evident that Suleiman had concentrated his forces into the sectors facing Aragon, England, Provence and Italy. The general assault was awaited.

At dawn on 24th September – 'even before the hour of morning prayer', say the Turkish accounts – the general bombardment opened with a screen of black smoke designed to blind the defenders. This time the Janissaries came first, led by their Agha, and were up and over the ramparts and had planted thirty or forty banners on the walls and the bastion of Aragon almost before the Knights had decided at what point the assault was to be expected.

From Aragon to Italy the Muslim pressed forward, heedless of the hail of fire from traverses and roof-tops, until they were up to the retrenchments and palisades which Tadini had constructed well inside the original enceinte. L'Isle Adam was everywhere, his banner of the Crucifixion following, and wherever he appeared the enemy seemed to waver and fall back.

The Rhodian civilians behaved magnificently: the men fighting with any weapon that came to hand, the women carrying powder and balls, hauling cannon, fetching food and water, and tending the wounded. One woman, whose name has not survived, the mistress of an English Knight, was so moved to frenzy at the sight of her lover's corpse – and so sure that if he were dead, all must be lost – that she killed her children to save them from apostasy, and, donning the dead Knight's corselet, rushed with his sword into the thick of the Janissaries. They were so taken aback at the sight of this avenging Fury with her flying tresses, that several had fallen to her inexpert hand before she was cut down.[29]

Once more the Franciscans, inspired by the memory of their warrior confrere Julius II, excelled themselves, comforting the dying in the blood-soaked ruins at one moment, and laying manfully about them with mace or pike at the next. For six hours the combat swayed backwards and forwards, from rampart to ditch and from ditch to retrenchment.

Jacques de Bourbon was selected to recover the bastion of Aragon. He tells how he entered by a countermining tunnel and made his way up, with a picked body of men-at-arms, on to the barbican. The Turkish banners were still flying – above piles of Turkish dead. Only two or three men were alive. The guns of Auvergne had killed the rest.

Nicholas Roberts wrote to the Earl of Surrey:

> Eury one of the IIII governours under the gret Turk . . . made a breche in the wall of the towne; that in some places Vc. men on horseback myght come in at once; and after that the wall of the towne was downe, they gave us battall often tymes upon even ground, that we had no manner of advantage apone them; yet thankid be God and Saint John, at euvry battall they returned without their purpose.

At length the roar of the cannon and the crack of the handguns, the screams and groans of the dying, the shouted war-cries, the hissing of the seething pitch, the ring of steel on steel, diminished. No more threats, or promises, no visions of paradise could induce the Muslim to return to the broken walls over tumbled rubble slippery with blood, behind which the ironclad Franks – veritable spirits of Eblis – still stood.

Suleiman had caused a raised platform to be erected within full view of the fighting. He was dismayed and very angry. The full weight of his fury descended upon Mustafa, who had promised an easy victory. It was now almost four months since the conquering armada had set out. The last three assaults had been immensely costly. The Beys of Tekke and Valona were amongst the dead. He condemned Mustafa to death. Pir Pasha, the eldest of the Vezirs, begged him to be merciful, but Suleiman condemned him to death, also, and Ayas Pasha was put in chains. But all the Pashas now begged the Sultan not to do this thing which would give so much cause for rejoicing to the Kuffar. Suleiman relented;

but Mustafa was relieved of the chief command and his rival Ahmed replaced him.[30]

However, the Christians were in bad shape. They had lost at the very least another 200 of their front line, and 150 more were disabled from wounds. Bourbon had been wounded, Fra François de Fresnay, the Commander of Romagna, had been killed, as had the English Turcopilier, Fra John Buck, and the German Fra Christopher Waldners. Many others had died of wounds. Jean de Letoux had lost an arm and William Weston a finger of his sword hand. These were but a few of the more senior casualties. The losses of Servants-at-Arms, men-at-arms, mercenaries, militia and of indispensable slave labour, must have added up to many more than are anywhere recorded. And the garrison was running out of repair materials, notably timber, to make good bombardment and mining damage. There were fears – though groundless as yet – of famine.

Mustafa, still in disgrace with the Sultan and reduced in rank, but anxious to demonstrate his continuing zeal, tried to mount fresh assaults against England during the last days of September. There were bombardments, and *carcasses* were fired into the Jews' Quarter; but Bourbon was told by a deserter that 'nothing could move Mustafa's troops to return to that bastion. It was folly to die for the caprice of a Commander'. Mustafa was soon to disappear from the scene. Vertot remarked[31] that 'had Mustafa been as well followed by his soldiers as his courage deserved, Rhodes would have been in great danger [from the attack of 24th September]. . . .'

On 30th September news reached Suleiman of the birth of a son, and the besiegers relaxed for a few hours to celebrate. On 4th October, at midnight, an enemy tunnel under the rampart of Italy was demolished by Tadini, killing a number of Azab. During the same night Fra Jean de Bressolx arrived from Naples with assurances of the early dispatch of a relief force.

There was, in fact, a relief force assembling at Messina. But it was too late in the season. The winds were already contrary – a sufficient excuse for the faint-hearted and the lukewarm. An English relief force commanded by Fra Thomas Newport, the Bailiff of Egle, carrying a body of seasoned English troops, sailed

Gabriele Tadini da Martinengo, from a painting
by an unknown artist

L'Isle Adam leaves Rhodes on New Year's Day, 1523, from a fresco by Mateo Perez de Alesio in the Palace, Malta

from Dover in mid-October. They were wrecked in the Bay of Biscay and lost with all hands.

It was now intensely cold, with frosty nights, and there was snow on the mountains. The winds were easterly, and there was sickness in the Turkish lines; but Ahmed continued the work of widening the breaches by bombardment and by under-mining, of silencing the city's batteries, and of launching continuous, costly assaults on the key bastions of Aragon and England. In one of these, Bali Agha, the Commander of the Janissaries, was badly wounded and put out of action.

There were only two serviceable cannon remaining in the ruins of the tower of Aragon – at the lowest level, where they were screened from the fire of the Turkish batteries on the earthworks. Tadini recommended the demolition of the tower to provide masonry for the retrenchments which he was continually building in the city. Soon the guns of Auvergne and at the Gate of Koskino were the only danger to the advancing Turks and to the working parties busy with their bores under the English bastion and covered by screens of hides. Casualties were still horrifying; but Ahmed was not the man to let that deter him. The Azab were not only expendable, but replaceable.

On 11th October a calamity befell the Knights. Gabriele Tadini was shot in the right eye, the ball passing clean through the side of his head and out by the ear.[32] He was out of action for six weeks. At four points, the ravelins, ramparts and curtains of the posts of Aragon, England, Provence and Italy had been breached or by-passed underground, and the city was open. But with the exception of that of Aragon, the towers and bastions at each post, in varying stages of damage, still stood and were still capable of murderous flanking fire. At the same time, facing each breach, Tadini had created strong retrenchments so that the besiegers had themselves been compelled to erect parapets across the opening of each breach. Here, with a stretch of level ground separating them, the contestants watched each other through embrasures in the improvised defences. Tadini had been peering through an embrasure when an alert musketeer had picked him off.

The weakest point was the English bastion, and it was here that 'there was the greatest bloodshed . . . the warmest attacked and withal the best defended'.[33] From all sources (and King's trans-literation of English names), the following Englishmen fought at Rhodes in 1522: John Buck (killed), Henry Mansell (killed), Thomas Sheffield (killed), Nicholas Hussey, William Weston, Nicholas Roberts, Nicholas Fairfax, John Rawson, Giles Russell, John Baron, Francis Bluett, Thomas Pemberton, George Askew, John Sutton, George Aylmer, all wounded. Michael Roche, an Irishman whose kinsman had fought in 1480, seems to have survived unwounded. Thomas Newport was lost with his ship on passage with a relief force. There were doubtless many other, less distinguished, English, Scottish and Irish casualties.

By October most of the English Langue were dead or disabled. The Frenchman Jean Bin de Malincorne had been put in command of the post of England, now manned largely by reserves from the other seven Langues.

On 14th October a brigantine arrived from Naples by way of Candia, bringing four Italian Knights and a recruit – the young nephew of the Bailiff of San Stefano, Giovanni di Gesualdo – seeking admission to the Holy Religion. He was admitted on 15th October, and killed in a sortie on the 16th.

Twenty men-at-arms and four trained gunners had arrived from Candia on the 15th. On the 16th, Fra Robert de Roque Martine, Lieutenant of the Commander of St. Peter, arrived seeking news of the Convent. He was sent back to fetch men and munitions.

On 20th October twelve men-at-arms and 'two good master sappers' arrived from Lindos. L'Isle Adam was now facing the necessity of abandoning the outposts. But he could not get from them what he lacked most – labour.

A muster of stocks of munitions – powder and balls and shot, arrows and bolts – showed that they must be conserved, and L'Isle Adam ordered that no weapons were to be fired against the enemy except by the specific order of a senior officer. The order was not solely meant to conserve stocks. He was worried, too, by fresh stories of messages being fired into the Turkish lines by Rhodians. A distinguished and brave Rhodian citizen, Lucio Castrofilaco, took exception to the order and stated his intention of disobeying it if he saw fit. Stories of treachery and of the existence of a fifth column spread like a plague. Castrofilaco was tried, put to the question and hanged for treason. A Turkish slave-woman who was said to have plotted to start fires in the city and, in the confusion, to open the gates was also hanged.

It was towards the end of the morning watch on 27th October. The look-out on the tower of St. George, in the post of Auvergne, was huddled in his cloak against the damp chill of the sea fog which still hung over the battlements and the Turkish trenches and the lower slopes of Mount St. Stephen. It had rained heavily for two days, washing away much of the great earthworks with their batteries before the English bastion, and driving the Turks out of their advance positions on the counterscarp. His eye caught a movement on the ramparts below. Another cloaked figure was bending over, winding the cranequin of a crossbow. The look-out ran down and apprehended the man just as he was raising the loaded bow to his shoulder. It was one Blasco Diaz, a Portuguese Jewish convert in the service of the Prior of Castile, the Chancellor, Andrea D'Amaral, whom he had served for many years since his ransom from Turkish captivity, as valet and body-servant. To the flat-headed bolt which Diaz had been about to fire a message was attached, addressed to Ayas Pasha.

At his preliminary investigation Diaz was silent; but when put to the question, the cords of the rack were scarcely tight before he volunteered a full confession, pleading that he was carrying out the orders of the Chancellor, as he had done on several previous occasions. The present message urged the Turks not to abandon the siege now. The condition of the garrison, it said, was desperate. Powder and shot were running low. There was sufficient for one more assault. The people were on the point of insurrection. If terms were offered, L'Isle Adam would be compelled to accept. Diaz added that his master had been in constant communication with the Sultan's people since long before the siege.

As the news of the arrest of Diaz spread, witnesses began to come forward by the dozen – all anxious to ensure the downfall of the arrogant and unpopular D'Amaral. The city was full of rumours of treason. A half-mad Spanish 'prophetess' was roaming the streets bare-footed and dishevelled, screaming doom and calling down the wrath of God upon the heads of traitors in high places. The Jew, Apella Renato, had been arrested, tried and convicted of firing messages into the enemy lines. Castrofilaco had been executed on the mere suspicion that he might do the same. D'Amaral was arrested by order of L'Isle Adam and confined in the Tower of St. Nicholas.

A priest of the Greek rite deposed that some weeks earlier he had seen D'Amaral, with Diaz, upon the walk-way of Auvergne. Diaz had a crossbow in his hand, and the Chancellor had made as if to screen his servant from view, asking the priest 'what he did there at that hour' and ordering him away. The priest had not reported the incident because he was afraid of the Chancellor.

A senior Knight of D'Amaral's own Langue deposed that, after the announcement of L'Isle Adam's election in January 1521, D'Amaral had remarked in his hearing: 'He [L'Isle Adam] will be the last Grand Master of Rhodes.'[34] Other Castilian and Portuguese Knights confirmed the statement, and added that D'Amaral had also announced that 'he would sell his soul to the Devil if he could encompass the ruin of the Order and L'Isle Adam with it'.

A Candiot woman said that Diaz had told her that D'Amaral had long been plotting with the Vezirs to hand over Rhodes, and that he had made away with stocks of gunpowder and had deliberately misinformed the Council about the original supplies. Some of the Italian Knights deposed that D'Amaral had incited three of their number to desert the Convent in the spring, on the pretext of journeying to complain about the improper disposal of benefices.

By modern standards, it is doubtful whether a prima facie case existed against the Chancellor. The evidence of Diaz would be inadmissible, having been obtained under torture or threat of torture. The evidence of D'Amaral's outburst at the announcement of L'Isle Adam's election – even if admissible at all, which is doubtful – might collapse altogether in cross-examination, and part at least of it, shorn of imagination or exaggeration, is capable of a wholly innocent interpretation. The evidence of the Greek priest might, without much difficulty, be shown to be malicious and false. The evidence of the Italian Knights that D'Amaral incited or encouraged three of them to leave the Convent at a time of peril, even if true, amounts to very little but an error of judgement. The evidence about the stock of powder is highly improbable.

In fact, we do not know the names of any witnesses except Diaz. We do not know for certain what court actually tried the Chancellor. All we do know is that D'Amaral was arrested by order of the Grand Master, interrogated and put to the question.

It has been said that Fontanus was one of D'Amaral's judges. He was a judge of the Appellate Court of Rhodes, and his record of the siege displays remarkable reticence about D'Amaral's trial. The most likely court to have tried the Chancellor was the special military tribunal set up by L'Isle Adam at the commencement of the siege.

The Chancellor appears to have made little or no attempt to defend himself. He was a man of iron courage, impetuous, an outstanding leader who had served the Order devotedly for forty years at sea and on land. He was also ambitious, arrogant, a fierce disciplinarian, with few friends and a great many enemies.

We need not doubt that D'Amaral disliked L'Isle Adam and resented his election, and that both men remembered their quarrel before the battle of Laiazzo in 1510.[35] But at least part of D'Amaral's outburst at the election of his old rival could have been a perfectly natural and not inaccurate prediction, i.e. the words 'he will be the last Grand Master of Rhodes'. The Chancellor, like any other intelligent and reasonably well-informed observer, knew that after the fall of Constantinople Rhodes had been fortunate by every human standard to survive at all. He knew, too, that a crusade was improbable, that Turkish sea-power was growing daily, and that with the conquest of Egypt there were no longer two Muslim powers in the eastern Mediterranean who might be played one against the other. He knew that the Papacy was virtually powerless, Venice complaisant, France and Spain locked in a long struggle for supremacy, and Italy constantly racked by civil war. He knew, none better, of the technical efficiency of Turkish artillery. And he knew that the teaching of Islam deprecated unnecessary slaughter. Every summons to surrender was similarly worded:

Accept Islam and live in peace under the Sultan: or deliver up the fortress and live in peace under the Sultan as Christian;

and if any man prefer let him depart peaceably taking his goods with him. But if you resist, then death, spoliation and slavery shall be the fate of you all.[36]

What if D'Amaral meant: 'He (thank the Lord!) and not I, will be the last Grand Master of Rhodes'?

The rest of this allegation – which Bourbon recounts with partisan emphasis – that D'Amaral had said 'he would sell his soul to the Devil if he could encompass the ruin of the Order and L'Isle Adam with it', is in the last degree improbable. What citizen – let alone a Knight – hearing the unpopular Chancellor give utterance to such plain treason, would have kept quiet about it? And if the Chancellor had ever said anything of this kind, is it likely, in a small, insulated Convent community, that the Grand Master would not come to hear of it, and, knowing it, would he then continue (as he did) to entrust the most important posts and the most essential military duties to a man who had – even in a fit of rage – uttered such sentiments?

But D'Amaral offered no explanation. Bourbon, who is our only contemporary witness of the trial apart from Fontanus, says, 'the Grand Master nominated two Grand Crosses to examine [the accused] together with the Judges of the Castellania. The traitor refused to confess. Confronted with his servant, D'Amaral denied everything and called him [Diaz] a poltroon. . . .'

Under torture, which he bore with unswerving fortitude, D'Amaral asserted that he had nothing to reveal, and reminded his questioners of the wounds he had suffered and the hardships he had borne during a lifetime of service to the Order. 'Am I, then, now to tell a lie and to sell my honour to save my old limbs from the pain of the rack?'[37]

As to the evidence of the priest, D'Amaral merely reminded him of the occasions upon which it had been necessary to rebuke him for his loose way of life. It is, anyway, difficult to accept the priest's story that he suspected something amiss at the time, but said nothing because he was afraid of D'Amaral. Had he said, 'I did not mention it because I thought nothing of it', we might more readily believe him.

As to the Candiot woman's corroboration of Diaz, even a sixteenth-century court might have hesitated before attaching weight to such evidence as: 'What he says must be true. He told me the same tale.' Diaz's own evidence – making due allowance for torture, or the fear of it – does not seem like a complete tissue of lies; but whether the court was justified in accepting it in its entirety may be another matter.

The truth about the 'gunpowder plot' is not far to seek. The three Commissioners – the Frenchman Fra Gabriel de Pommerols, the Englishman Fra John Buck, and D'Amaral himself – had little or no comparable experience to guide them. The use of artillery in siege warfare was not new, but the power and effectiveness of cannon and hand-guns changed and improved constantly. The quantity of powder and shot likely to be used was hard to predict, and it varied with the range desired and the weight of shot. The countermining operations of Tadini, although eminently success-ful, must also have consumed an unpredictable amount of explo-sive. Further, for reasons of wind and weather – the prevailing winds change from westerly to north-easterly in November and gales and rain and hail-storms are common: no weather for sitting in entrenchments with your supply lines to the mainland menaced by contrary winds – it was to be expected that the siege, if it could be held off during the long summer, would be abandoned as the winter approached. In this matter D'Amaral and his fellow Commissioners were guilty of no more than poor logistics – a commonplace of all wars.

As to the suggestion that D'Amaral actually made away with some of the stocks of munitions: how could this have been done without the complicity of his fellow Commissioners? How could it have been done physically? At dead of night, perhaps, with the aid of slaves? Under some pretext or other, officially? But certainly not without a considerable number of persons being aware of the operation – and what slave, with an op-portunity of turning 'Grand Master's evidence', would have kept silent?

Attempts to lend colour to the gunpowder story have been made by later writers pointing to the explosion of a quantity of powder, said to have been stored in the crypt of the church of St. John, during a thunderstorm in 1856. There was, in fact, an earthquake in that year and a great many of the surviving build-ings of the Order were destroyed;[38] but the presence of gunpowder in a crypt or cellar after three centuries of Turkish rule can scarcely be attributed to D'Amaral.

The surviving archives of the Order contain no record of the trial. The *Acta Consiliorum* were not kept during 1480 or 1522. Bourbon is violently partisan. He says that even before the siege, D'Amaral:

> . . . incited the Turks to attack . . .
>
> . . . conceived an implacable hatred against the Order and against L'Isle Adam . . .
>
> . . . informed Suleiman of the affairs of the Order and of the condition of the City . . . and that a part of the enceinte had been demolished for reconstruction . . . that a number of the Knights were in a state of mutiny, stirred up by him, and that the Christian Princes were too much involved to be able to aid the Order . . .
>
> . . . sent a Turkish prisoner with messages for Suleiman to Constantinople, upon whose return everyone was surprised but no-one dared speak of it . . .

'Everyone' knew, apparently, except the Grand Master and D'Amaral's colleagues on the Council. A likely story!

We are left with the impression that Bourbon was repeating all the stories which were current about D'Amaral after the event. He does preface his report with the explanation that 'in the course of the siege, I was never absent from Rhodes; but it was not possible for me to be present at every event; nevertheless I only write of matters which I have learned from persons of good repute, whose reports are not less true than if I had seen the things with my own eyes'. We must accept that he wrote what he believed to be true.

Fontanus says remarkably little about the trial. Speaking of the Commissioners and referring to the death in action of the French-man and the Englishman, he says that 'the third was destined by God for a more terrible fate'.

The Grand Master himself must have believed D'Amaral guilty. He wrote to his nephew, Anne de Montmorency, Marshal of France, on 13th November 1522 thus:

> . . . Mon nepveu, je vous advise que je n'ay pas eu la guerre

seullement avec les Turcqs, mais avec l'ung des plus grants de notre conseil, lequel par envie et ambicion de dominer, des longtemps avait conspire fair venir le Turcq et promis lui rendre cette cite. Le cas a este divinement manifeste et avere et ila este exequte comme plus a plain serez informe par notre Chevalier frere Mery de Ruyaulx, porteur de la presente a qui vous plaira donner creance. . . .[39]

. . . I tell you, my Nephew, that I have not been at war only with the Turks, but with one of the most senior members of our Council who, by reason of envy and a thirst for power, had long conspired to bring the Turk here and had promised to surrender this city to him. The matter has been divinely revealed and confirmed and he has been executed, all of which will be made more plain to you by our Brother the Chevalier Mery de Ruyaulx, who brings this present and to whose report you may give credence. . . .

L'Isle Adam and Bourbon were convinced of D'Amaral's guilt. Bourbon's allegation that D'Amaral was responsible for persuading the Turks to continue the siege after they had decided to abandon it is emphatic. He says that 'his treachery was more horrible than that of Judas, because his resulted in the ultimate good of mankind; but D'Amaral's was the principal cause of the loss of Rhodes'.

Although the evidence was that Diaz had been prevented from firing the vital message on 27th October, Bourbon assumes that Ayas Pasha had received it and that preparations for striking camp had already commenced when he carried the message to Suleiman, who then reversed his decision to abandon the siege. Turkish evidence suggests that the Sultan was already determined to keep his army before the city throughout the winter. Mustafa Gelal-Zade tells us that on 28th October Mustafa Pasha handed over the command of his sector to Qasim Pasha on receipt of the news of the death of Khair Bey, the Governor of Egypt, whom he succeeded. There would have been little point in transferring the command of a sector of the lines if the siege was about to be lifted. Fighting continued with great violence on 29th October. Again, there would have been no point in losing further lives in assaults if retreat was already intended. On 31st October

Suleiman announced to a full council of his Vezirs his intention to continue the siege at all costs. Preparations for wintering in the lines commenced and the fleet was sent to anchor in Marmarice.

Continental historians of the Holy Religion have followed Bourbon, and D'Amaral has been represented as the arch-traitor. British narrators, like Porter and Sutherland, Townsend and King, tend to think D'Amaral innocent, or, at least, to give him the benefit of the doubt. They are, perhaps, subconsciously applying the English principle of 'innocent until proved guilty'.

Trionfi has created a splendidly dramatic encounter between Villiers de L'Isle Adam and Andrea D'Amaral. The accused has been brought from his cell in the Tower of St. Nicholas, and the two of them are alone together in the Grand Master's private apartment. L'Isle Adam begs his old comrade-in-arms to say something in his defence and is answered only by an obstinate and arrogant silence. He knows, Villiers says, that torture will not make Andrea speak if he is determined not to; but in the name of their common faith in the Holy Trinity, in Our Lady and St. John, in the name of their Holy Religion, in the name – if nothing else will move him – of Andrea's own honour, he, the Grand Master, is begging him to speak. At last D'Amaral is moved to a furious outburst in which he confesses everything with which he is charged, and more. 'It is true,' he says, 'that I would sell my soul to the Devil if only I could encompass the ruin of Villiers de L'Isle Adam, and, because he is their ruler, of the Order and of the City. . . .'

There are other highly dramatic possibilities. D'Amaral may have been so soundly hated that his own servant and his own confreres welcomed an opportunity of disposing of him. He may have been the victim of a complicated fifth column, rather than its leader.

It is not easy to make a case for D'Amaral. His own silence does not help, but it may be that the best case would not have saved his life. No matter how unreliable and biased much of the evidence for the prosecution was, the balance of probability indicated that he had been in communication with the enemy more than once. No statement in mitigation, pleading the excellence of his intentions, could have changed the finding. He was found guilty, stripped of his habit and of all his honours, carried in a chair to the place of execution – for he had been so sorely racked that he could not walk – where, arrogant to the end, he waved away all offers of spiritual comfort. His head and the quartered members of his body were displayed upon different parts of the battlements, spitted upon pikes, on 8th November. Diaz had suffered, by hanging, on 6th November.

It may be that D'Amaral was guilty of no more than failure to support L'Isle Adam's determination, in the absence of a relief force from the west, to die in the ruins of Rhodes. In this D'Amaral was not alone. He shared with the Grand Master and with others a determination that the Order should survive at whatever cost to himself; but he and others differed as to means.

L'Isle Adam believed that by sacrificing every Knight, every man, woman and child in Rhodes he might, in the last battle amongst the flaming ruins, inflict such terrible losses upon the Turk, and light so bright a torch, that Christendom would be revived by its light and the Order would survive to lead a great new crusade.

D'Amaral, on the other hand, believed that a temporary accommodation with the Ottomans would enable the Order to seek new empires for the Cross in that wider world which his compatriots had opened across the Atlantic and the Indian Ocean. D'Amaral knew that Europe would never again unite to make war on the Ottomans; and in his communication with an enemy who had shown that, for all his occasional barbarities, he could be magnanimous and not unreasonable, he intended peace with honour. To have made a truce with Islam would not have been anything new or shocking. While Djem had lived as an honoured hostage under D'Aubusson, the Order had enjoyed several years of something approaching amity with the Sultan Bajazet.

So to a clash of personalities was added a clash of policy. L'Isle Adam represented the old, pre-renaissance crusading spirit of St. Louis; D'Amaral the new spirit of Machiavelli's Prince, 'who must not sacrifice his country to his sense of honour, nor accept, for the sake of a code that no one else will observe, the contemptuous appellation of "Ser Nihilo"'. It was D'Amaral's tragedy that peace with honour was exactly what L'Isle Adam was to achieve while the Chancellor's dishonoured bones were still crow's meat upon the walls.

On 9th November reinforcements arrived from St. Peter in two brigantines carrying twelve Knights and 100 men-at-arms. There were also welcome supplies of victuals and powder and shot.

On the 14th Fra Nicholas Fairfax sailed for Candia where he was to rendezvous with a party of volunteers and collect a carrack and a barque which had been secretly laden with provisions. Fra Emeric Depreaulx left for Naples where he was to make one more effort to enlist help.

On 15th November two barques from Lindos arrived with munitions and twelve Knights. On the 16th a galley sailed for Kos to fetch more reinforcements from the garrison there.

Meanwhile, the Turks were burrowing their way deeper and deeper into the city. They were under the retrenchments and beyond; but Tadini's mine-watchers were alert, and counter-mining and trenching went on in spite of the shortage of labour and of timber for shores and props. In places, only the thickness of a plank separated the Rhodian miners from their enemies.

On 21st November there were attacks which gained a foothold on the bastions of England and Italy; but after fierce fighting the Turks were once more beaten back to their flooded trenches, and there was a respite of some days while rain and hail and bitter easterly gales swept over the island.

On 30th November there was another general assault which Nicholas Roberts reports:

> Upon Saint Andrue ys evin last, was the last batall that was between the turkes and vs; at that batall was slain XI thousand turkes, and of our part, a hundred and four score, and after that day the turkes purposed to give us no more batall, but to come into the towne by trenches in so much, yt they mad [many] gret trenches, and by the space of a month did come allmost into the mydst of our towne, in so much that ther lay nightly wtin our towne [many] thousand turkes.

On 1st December Tadini, now fit again, led a sortie against the sappers in the ditch, who were boring yet more tunnels beneath the post of Aragon. He was badly wounded in the knee by a scimitar. The bastions of Italy and England were already so undermined that it was marvellous that they stood at all.

On 3rd December a Genoese merchant, one Girolamo Monile, appeared at the Gate of Koskino under a flag of truce and exhorted the defenders to surrender, assuring them that Suleiman would spare their lives. He was ordered away. Two days later Monile appeared again, this time on the pretext that he wished to speak to a distinguished compatriot in the city, Matteo de Via. Told that de Via was sick, he said that what he really wanted was to deliver a letter from the Sultan to the Grand Master. Once more he was told to take himself off, and a shot was fired over his head to hasten his going. The next day an Albanian envoy appeared at the gate. He, too, was ordered away.

All this low-level manœuvring seems to have been designed, either by Ahmed or by Suleiman himself, to avoid loss of face in appearing to offer terms. But the news that there had been some kind of approach was soon known throughout the city. The citizens, says Bourbon, 'cared more about themselves and their families than about honour'. They dared not take any overt step, but they approached their bishops, Balestrieri and Clement, and they in turn enlisted the sympathy of some of the Conventual Bailiffs, who went in a body to L'Isle Adam and represented that if he was not prepared to negotiate with Suleiman, there was a danger that the townspeople would rebel and attempt to make a separate peace.

The Grand Master had long since determined to resist to the death. If he was apt to be cautious, he was also uncommonly stubborn. But he was persuaded to summon the Council. The gallant Prior of St. Gilles, Prejan de Bidoux, reported that there was no more labour for moving cannon or repairing defences. All the slaves were dead, wounded or sick. Powder and shot were almost exhausted. There was no hope of saving the city. Tadini pointed out that the enemy were already in the city, both above and below ground. He agreed that the city was beyond saving. Fra Lopes de Pas of the Langue of Aragon urged the Grand Master not to 'make the enemy's victory the more splendid by our deaths. . . .' 'As to succour from Europe,' he went on, 'either it will not come at all, or it will be too little and, by failing at the first encounter with Suleiman, will merely worsen our condition.

... Where all human hope is gone, it is our duty to try to come to terms, so that we may vindicate our loss at another time and place. . . . Wise men surrender to necessity. No matter how praiseworthy our death, let us consider whether it may not be more damaging to the Holy Religion than our surrender.'[40]

It might almost have been Macchiavelli – or D'Amaral – speaking. Suddenly, there came a hammering at the locked doors of the council chamber. A deputation of Rhodians, suspicious that the Knights might decide on some course which ignored the interests of the townspeople, had appeared – 'weeping and begging (an old method of argument with the Rhodians)', says Pantaleone, unjustly in the circumstances.

Nicholas Roberts puts the Rhodian case:

'The Commons of the towne hearing this gret proffer (of the gret Turk to give us our lyves and our goodes) came to the Lord Master and said that considering that the walle and strength of the towne ys taken, and the municons spent, and the most of yor Knights and men slaine, and allso seeing ther is no soccours redy to come, they determined [to take] this partido that the gret Turk geveth us the lyves of our wiffes and children. The Lord Master hering the opinion of the hole commonalty resolved to take that partido, fell downe almost ded, and what time he recoveryd himsel in sort, he seeing them contenue in the same, at last consented to the same.

On 10th December Suleiman ordered the white flag to be hoisted on the tower of the church of Our Lady of Mercy, within the Turkish lines, thus by Turkish convention inviting the Christians to surrender, and either to live in peace under Islam, retaining their religion, or else to depart unharmed. L'Isle Adam replied with a white flag over one of the towers of the Koskino Gate, outside which there very shortly appeared two Turkish envoys[41] – the nephew of Ahmed Pasha, and the Sultan's official interpreter. They were received by the Prior of St. Gilles and Tadini,[42] to whom they delivered a letter from the Sultan in which he demanded the surrender of the city, and promised that the Grand Master and all his Order would be allowed to leave in peace, taking with them all their personal property and any citizens who wished to follow them. Should the terms prove unacceptable, the Sultan swore to massacre every soul in Rhodes, and he demanded a prompt and unequivocal reply.

L'Isle Adam once more summoned the Council. Suleiman's terms were accepted and on 11th December Fra Antoine de Grollée and a judge of the Rhodian Court, one Roberto Peruzzi, were dispatched to the pavilion of Ahmed Pasha, charged to ask for a truce of three days to allow the Grand Master to make his arrangements for a final surrender and to clarify the terms. The envoys were taken to Suleiman, who denied having made any written offer – as a matter of form – and then repeated his terms. He granted the request for a truce, but added that no work on the defences or warlike dispositions of any kind were to be undertaken during the three days. On 12th December Peruzzi returned to the city; but Grollée was kept by Ahmed as a hostage, and courteously entertained. The two men discussed the fighting, and Ahmed is supposed to have volunteered the information that the Turks had lost '64,000 men, killed and dead of wounds, and a further 50,000 from sickness', figures which are incredible. Almost as incredible was the astonishing toughness of these men, on both sides, who survived wounds – punctured lungs, shattered limbs, shots in the eye – of which most men today would die even with all the help of modern medicine. Yet there is no doubt that they did survive.

L'Isle Adam and the Council had doubts about Suleiman's offer. They could, perhaps, trust his word; but the terms would need to be a good deal more specific before Ahmed and the Janissaries could be trusted. The Rhodians shared these doubts, and a deputation of the younger, hotter-headed citizens waited on L'Isle Adam to represent that, if what they had heard from Peruzzi were true, the interests of the native Rhodians and their families and property were not adequately protected. If Ahmed intended to massacre the townspeople after the Order had left, to destroy their churches and enslave their families, then it would be better to fight on – and to die fighting. The Grand Master was very ready to agree with their last sentiment; but he assured them that he intended to exact a promise from the Sultan ensuring the safety of the citizens before he gave up the city.

The truce was to expire on 15th December. Turkish accounts

allege that L'Isle Adam was playing for time and that the request for a truce was to enable expected reinforcements to arrive.[43]

On the 14th Fra Raimondo Marquet and Fra Lopes de Pas were sent to Ahmed to ask for a further audience with Suleiman, and to say that L'Isle Adam needed more time to refer the terms of the surrender to his many different subjects – the Knights of eight different nations, the Frankish settlers, and the native Greeks of Rhodes. Suleiman was sure that the Grand Master was temporizing. Even before the arrival of the fresh envoys, so the Turks claimed, the truce had been broken by the Christians. Two wretched Christian soldiers were caught transporting earth in Ahmed's sector. They had their noses and ears cut off and were sent to L'Isle Adam with an insolent and abusive letter. A gunner in the post of Auvergne could not resist firing at a distinguished-looking Turk who was parading on the counterscarp.

On the 15th Suleiman ordered the resumption of the attack. The guns opened up all along the lines. The garrison replied – though feebly, for they had little powder.

L'Isle Adam was not displeased at the breakdown of the negotiations. He sent for the Rhodian representatives and ordered them to muster their people at the barricades and on the broken walls – now, he said, was their opportunity to redeem their warlike promises of a few days since. They obeyed; but in spite of the public execution of one of their number who deserted his post, after two or three days they began to go off to their houses.

On 16th December Nicholas Fairfax returned from Candia with a few troops and a cargo of wine. He had had difficulties with the Venetians but had finally left Crete on the pretext of taking passage for Sicily with some wine which was destined for Flanders; once at sea, he had seized the carrack and brought her into Rhodes. 'For two months,' wrote Bourbon, 'we had drunk nothing but water' – a less comfortable assertion than it seems, for the sixteenth century regarded wine as a necessity, and water (justifiably) as dangerous to health.

On the 17th and 18th the Turks made a half-hearted attack through the breaches of Aragon and England, but they were beaten back from the retrenchments. The Holy Religion had fought Islam to a standstill.

The Rhodians were now almost in open revolt. They demanded to be allowed to appoint envoys of their own choice and selected Nicolo Vergonti and Pietro Sincritico to treat on their behalf. These two, with de Grollée, were presented to Suleiman by Ahmed, who had meanwhile strongly advised L'Isle Adam against attempting to influence Suleiman by producing Bajazet's treaty with D'Aubusson of 1482.

On 24th December the Turkish guns were once more silent. Suleiman was now willing not only to let the Holy Religion depart with honour, but to furnish them with ships if their own did not suffice. He repeated his promises to protect the lives and property of the citizens, and added that they should be free to leave his domain at any time up to three years hence. Twelve days were allowed within which the Order and its followers and dependents must leave.

Twenty-five Knights, including two Grand Crosses, were to be sent as hostages to the Turkish lines, with twenty-five prominent citizens. Four hundred Janissaries were to enter the city at once as guards. The rest of the investing troops were to be withdrawn to a line one mile from the counterscarp.

Suleiman and L'Isle Adam met three times. What passed between them is largely hearsay; but all European reports agree that the Sultan was courteous, almost warm. Nicholas Roberts was one of the hostages and also met him. He found Suleiman 'very wise and discreet'.

On 26th December L'Isle Adam went to make his submission and presents were exchanged, the Grand Master offering a sum of money in gold pieces, and receiving a richly embroidered cloak. As he left, Suleiman turned to Ibrahim Pasha, his Grand Vezir, and said: 'It saddens me to be compelled to cast this brave old man out of his home.' On the 27th, Suleiman returned the Grand Master's call, riding into Rhodes through the Gate of St. John, and insisting on dismissing his guard, saying, 'My safety is guaranteed by the word of a Grand Master of the Hospitallers, which is more sure than all the armies in the world.'[44]

Accounts of Turkish behaviour differ. Fontanus says that they 'forced the Koskino Gate and entered arrogantly, profaning all the churches and dedicating them to Mahomet. The Christians were used like draught animals and some slain. Statues of Christ were soiled with filth and citizens publicly insulted'. Pantaleone says that the Order and its followers were allowed to take away all their arms, except their bronze cannon, and their possessions, with the Sacred Relics of the True Cross, the Holy Thorn, the Right Hand of St. John, and part of the Precursor's Skull, the Holy Body of St. Euphemia and other less notable objects of veneration. There was also the Holy Ikon of Our Lady of Phileremos, which travelled with the Order to Malta, where it remained in the Conventual Church of St. John until 1798.[45]

Mustafa Gelal-Zade says that the troops in the sectors of Pir and Ahmed entered the city on 24th December with the Agha and his Janissaries. On the 25th all the churches were converted into mosques and Christian images and symbols were defaced.

Bourbon says that the Turks beat and insulted the Christians, stripping some of their shirts; stole and committed sacrilege; dug up the tombs of the Grand Masters in a search for treasure, and raped some of the women. The Janissary guards also stole victuals and private property from the ships. When the Christians complained to Ahmed, he punished the looters and made them restore the stolen goods.

Bosio[46] also accuses the Turks of breaking the terms of the capitulation and of sacking the city. Pantaleone, on the other hand, says that they 'behaved with great humanity and scrupulously observed the terms of the surrender. They did not touch any of the sacred objects of the Holy Religion, and the Janissaries who entered the town with Suleiman were forbidden to utter a single insolent word'.

The worst behaved – as is often the way – were the fresh troops who had taken no part in the fighting and had arrived from Suleiman's eastern frontier after the capitulation.

On 27th December Suleiman received the keys of Kos and the fortress of Pheraclos. Murad, the son of the pretender Djem, and his grandson, who had been sent to Pheraclos for safe custody, were executed.[47] Murad's widow and his daughters were sent to Constantinople: an act of policy for which there were plenty of Christian precedents. The fortress of St. Peter – last foothold on the mainland of Asia – and the other outlying possessions of the Order were surrendered after L'Isle Adam had left Rhodes and Suleiman had left Marmarice on his homeward march. The remnants of the garrisons were given safe conducts and allowed to carry away their possessions.

In the early evening of 1st January 1523, L'Isle Adam, having taken leave of the Sultan and obtained a safe conduct from him, sailed for Candia with his personal standard in the carrack *Santa Maria*. With him were the galleys *Santa Caterina* and *San Giovanni*, a galleon, the *San Bonaventura* and a barque, the *Perla*. The flagship was commanded by the Englishman Sir William Weston.

Amongst the survivors who embarked with the Grand Master was a young Provençal called Jean Parisot de La Valette. Forty-three years later, when the remnant of his armies came back to Constantinople from the siege of Malta, beaten and shamed by the Grand Master La Valette, Suleiman was to regret his youthful act of chivalry in letting these accursed Kuffar escape alive.

At Candia the little fleet was delayed by bad weather, and the Knights rested and recovered from their wounds. In April L'Isle Adam reached Messina, and the cheering crowds, who greeted him like a victor, saw flying from his mainmast a rich banner bearing an image of Our Lady of Sorrows, with the votive inscription in Latin – 'Thou art the Sole Hope of the Afflicted'.[48] The more cynical might have added: 'Put not thy faith in Princes.'

Belloc's comment on the renaissance Papacy is peculiarly apposite to the fall of Rhodes:

> It was not the fault of the Papacy in its temporary decline and heavy spiritual lapse that the chief external task set to it – the saving of our civilization from armed attack – was not successful. The failure came from those Christian princes born into the old age of Mediaeval Civilization, or, rather born in its death agony. They could not or would not see in what peril we all lay – also, they did not care. . . .

When they told the Emperor-elect Charles V of the fall of Rhodes, he said: 'Nothing in the World was ever so well lost.'

EPILOGUE

On 2nd January 1523 the Sultan Suleiman led the faithful of Islam in public prayer in the new mosque which had been the Conventual Church of St. John. On the 29th he made his triumphal entry into Constantinople, having marched overland from Marmarice. In Rhodes he had left a garrison of 500 'fortress' troops and 500 Janissaries.[1] In due course Mehmed Bey, Governor of Mytilene, had the new Sanjak of Rhodes added to his territory.[2]

Three thousand Muslim of every condition had been liberated. Of the five or six thousand prisoners who had been employed as sappers and labourers, few survived.[3] As for the native Rhodians, Bourbon says that 'they lamented the piety, clemency and liberality of the Holy Religion and contrasted its rule with the impiety and avidity of the Turks. . . . Many fled to Cyprus, Crete and Italy. The more prominent citizens were taken away to Constantinople and new colonists brought in. . . .'

In Rhodes there is a tradition of a wholesale massacre after Suleiman had left, and they point to the Red Gate – the Gate of Koskino, or St. John – as one of the spots where the gutters ran red with Greek blood. Hence, they say, its name. But the Turkish records use the name 'Qizil Qapu', or Red Gate, as if the Turks were already calling it by that name during the siege; and this may well be a reference to the terrible slaughter dealt out by its batteries, which were never silenced.

It is true that all the Latin churches were converted into mosques. The Latin Bishop Balestrieri was sent into exile with the Knights;[4] but we know that there was a Greek Metropolitan in 1524, and some of the Greek churches must have survived. The Sultan Mehmet had promised his protection to the (schismatic) Greek Church in 1453.[5] Since most of the Latin settlers had left Rhodes with the Order, what need was there for Latin churches? It may be that Suleiman regarded his terms as applying differently to the Latin subjects of the Order and to the Greeks, whom he could, with some show of legality, regard as his own subjects.

Some three thousand Rhodians – not all of whom were Latin settlers[6] – were eventually to follow the Order, and many were to remain attached to L'Isle Adam in his wanderings and to settle in Malta.[7]

At Messina plague broke out in the Order's ships. After some weeks of quarantine, L'Isle Adam was invited by the Pope to bring the fleet – and the Convent – to Civita Vecchia, where he was joined by the fine new carrack *St. Anne*, which had been building at Marseilles.

In November 1523 Giulio de Medici, who had been a Hospitaller, was elected to the Papacy as Clement VII. He could be counted on to support his old Order in every way possible. But he had his own troubles. The temporal power of the Papacy itself was in peril, and in 1527 the enemies of Christendom were to be edified by the spectacle of Charles V's Lutheran Germans sacking Rome, murdering monks, and raping nuns. The Emperor Charles was less enthusiastic about the Holy Religion but, for once in agreement with the Pope, conceded that it not only deserved to survive but still had its uses, provided those were not in direct support of the Papacy.

L'Isle Adam's task was nothing less than a struggle to ensure the survival of the Order. All his old powers of charm, diplomacy and oratory were needed. He set off on a tour of the European capitals seeking support. Even Henry VIII of England, who, on the eve of the fall of Rhodes, had been imagining a scheme for the 'nationalization' of the English Langue and for using it to garrison Calais, gave him a useful gift of bronze cannon.

In the years from 1523 to 1530 the Order found temporary homes at Viterbo and at Nice; but the Knights would not readily accept the loss of Rhodes. The indispensable Antonio Bosio made several clandestine visits to the island in 1524, in an attempt to exploit Suleiman's troubles with Ahmed Pasha, who had scarcely waited to assume the Governorship of Egypt – in succession to his old rival Mustafa – before rebelling. Bosio was able to enlist the support of the Metropolitan Euthemios and the mutinous Agha of the Janissaries, and to get as far as smuggling arms into the potential insurgents; but nothing came of his plot.

In 1530 Charles was crowned Emperor. He offered Malta to

L'Isle Adam. A rare Chapter General[8] studied the report of the Commissioners sent to investigate the island. They found it 'merely a rock of soft sand-stone, called tufa, about six or seven leagues long and three or four broad', but with two great harbours. It was agreed reluctantly to accept the Emperor's offer of Malta and Tripoli.

But the Knights could not forget the snow-capped mountains and the green valleys of Rhodes. Malta, by comparison, was a desert only redeemed by its superb harbours and its soft, golden building stone. Yet, with Tripoli, it could be a splendid base from which to mount an expedition for the recovery of Rhodes.

In 1531 Bosio succeeded in contacting the Greek and Venetian dissidents in Ottoman-held Morea. The Captain of the Galleys, Fra Bernardo Salviati, nephew of the Pope and Prior of Rome, commissioned a force of four great galleys, chartered two more from Giacomo Grimaldi of Genoa and four brigantines from Malta, embarked a strong body of Knights and soldiers, and landed on the west coast of Morea at the end of August. The fortress and town of Modone (Methonis) were sacked, and 800 Turks taken prisoner with much rich spoil; but the Order had to retire before Ottoman reinforcements.

The vision of a successful assault and a re-occupation of Rhodes faded slowly. For twenty-one years the Order held Tripoli; an effort which bled them of men and treasure. Only after its loss in 1551 did the Order begin to reconcile itself to Malta. The measure of the reconciliation was to be the great siege of 1565.

THE HOSPITALLERS OF ST. JOHN

(Knights of Jerusalem, of Rhodes and of Malta)

A SHORT CHRONOLOGY

Hospital of the Abbot Probus in *Jerusalem*	... A.D.	600
Hospital of Charlemagne in *Jerusalem*	...	800
The Convent and Hospital of St. John in *Jerusalem*	...	1099
Hospitaller and Military Order of St. John at *Margat* (Lebanon)	...	1188
Hospitaller and Military Order of St. John at *St. Jean d'Acre* (Palestine)	...	1191
Hospitaller and Military Order of St. John at *Limassol* (Cyprus)	...	1291
Sovereign Military and Hospitaller Order of St. John in *Rhodes*	...	1309
Sovereign Order in *Messina, Nice, Viterbo* (temporary convents)	...	1523
Sovereign Order in *Malta*	...	1530
Sovereign Order in *Catania*	...	1798
Sovereign Order in *Ferrara*	...	1826
Sovereign Order in *Rome*	...	1834

Since the conquest of Rhodes in 1309, the Order has never relinquished its claim to sovereignty; a claim which is still recognized by thirty nations, including Malta, who maintain diplomatic relations with the Prince Grand Master in Rome.

The English Grand Priory suppressed by Henry VIII, restored by Mary Tudor and again suppressed by Elizabeth I, was revived, as a national Order, in 1831 and is now known as the Most Venerable Order of St. John of Jerusalem in the British Realm.

All branches of the Order are committed to the service of the poor and sick throughout the world.

BIBLIOGRAPHY

*(References in brackets are to abbreviations
used in the Notes and Text.)*

AENEAS SILVIUS, PIUS II, *Memoirs of a Renaissance Pope.* Trans.
F. A. Gragg and L. C. Gabel. London, 1960.   (Pius II)

Annales de L'Ordre Souverain Militaire de Malte. Palazzo Malta, Rome.
Periodical: references by number and author.   (A.O.S.M.)

ATIYA, AZIZ S., *Crusade, Commerce and Culture.* Indiana University,
1962.   (Atiya)

BELLOC, H., *How the Reformation happened.* London, 1964.   (Belloc)

BOSIO, G., *Dell'Istoria della Sacra Religione et Illma. Militia di San
Giovanni Gierosolimitano.* 3 vols, Rome, 1594.   (Bosio)

BOTTARELLI, G. and MONTERISI, M. *Storia Politica e Militare del
Sovrano Ordine di S. Giovanni.* 2 vols, Milan, 1940.   (Bottarelli)

BOUHOURS, FR. D., S. J., *Histoire de Pierre D'Aubusson.* Paris,
1676.   (Bouhours)

BOURBON, J. DE, *La Grande et Merveilleuse et très cruelle oppugnation
de la noble cité de Rhodes prinse naguères par Sultan Séliman à présent
Grand turcq, ennemy de la très sainte foy catholique redigée par escript
par excellent et noble chevalier Frère Jacques Bastard de Bourbon,
Commandent de Sainct Maulviz, Doysemont et Fonteynes au prieuré de
Paris.* Paris, 1526.   (Bourbon)

BOWLE, J., *Henry VIII.* London, 1964.   (Bowle)

BRADFORD, E., *Ulysses Found.* London, 1963.   (Bradford)

BURCHARD, JOHAN, *Johanni Burckardi Liber Notarum ab anno
MCCCCLXXXIII usque ad annum MDVI.* Trans. from the

Italian of Celani (Citta di Castello, 1906) by G. Parker. London, 1963. (Parker)

Cambridge New Modern History, vol. I. Cambridge, 1957. (C.N.M.H.)

CAOURSIN, W., *Obsidionis Rhodiae Urbis Descriptio.* Venice, 1480. English trans. by John Kaye, Laureate to King Edward IV, pub. by Caxton in 1496 under title: *The Dylectable newessee & Tithyngs of the Gloryoos Victorye of the Rhodyns Agaynst the Turkes.* (Caoursin)

CURTI, G. DE, *La Citta di Rodi assediata dai Turchi il di 23 maggio 1480.* Venice, 1480. (De Curti)

DUCAUT-BOURGET, F., *The Spiritual Heritage of the Sovereign Military Order of Malta.* Vatican, 1958. (D–B)

FINKE, H., *Acta Aragonesia.* Berlin, 1922. (Finke)

FISHER, H. A. L., *History of Europe.* London, 1936. (Fisher)

FONTANUS, J., (Jacob Fonteyn), *De Bello Rhodio.* Rome, 1524. (Fontanus)

GAUTIER, L., *Chivalry.* Trans. D. C. Dunning. London, 1965. (Gautier)

GONTARD, F., *The Popes.* London, 1964. (Gontard)

GILLE, B., *The Renaissance Engineers.* London, 1966. (Gille)

GRANCSAY, S. V., *Arms and Armour.* London, 1964. (Grancsay)

HAMMER, J. VON, *Geschichte des Osmanischen Reiches.* Trans. J. J. Hellert. Paris, 1841. (Hammer)

HOLLISTER, C. W., *The Military Organization of Norman England.* London, 1965. (Hollister)

HUGHES, P., *The Reformation.* London, 1957. (Hughes)

KING, E. J., *The Knights of St. John in England*. London, 1924. (King)

LAIRD-CLOWES, G. S., *Sailing Ships and their History*. London, 1923. (L–C)

Libri Conciliorum and *Libri Bullarum*. Records of S.M. Order of Malta in Royal Malta Library, Valletta. (Lib. Conc. and Lib. Bull.)

LYNCH, J., *Spain under the Habsburgs*. London, 1964. (Lynch)

Mediterranean Pilot, vol. IV. London, 1955. (Med. Pilot)

MULLER, J., *The Attack and Defence of Fortified Places*. London, 1770. (Muller)

Nouveau Dictionnaire Historique des Seiges et Batailles Memorables, vol. V., Paris, 1808. (N.D.H.)

PANTALEONE, E., *Militaris Ordinis Johannitarum Rhodiorum aut Melitensium Equitum.* 12 vols, Basle, 1581. (Pantaleone)

PARKER, G., *see under* Burchard.

PAULI, S., *Codice Diplomatico del S.M. Ordine Gerosolimitano*. 2 vols, Lucca, 1737. (Pauli)

PORTER, W., *The Knights of Malta*. 2 vols, London, 1883. (Porter)

PROMIS, C., *Biografie di Ingegneri Militari Italiani*. Turin, 1874. (Promis)

ROSSI, E., *Storia della Marina dell'Ordine di San Giovanni*. Rome, 1927. (Rossi I)

ROSSI, E., *Assedio e Conquista di Rodi nel 1522 secondo le relazioni edite ed inedite dei Turchi*. Rome, 1927. (Rossi II)

ROWSE, A. L., *The Expansion of Elizabethan England*. London, 1955. (Rowse)

RUNCIMAN, S., *The Fall of Constantinople*. Cambridge, 1965. (Runciman)

SALLES, F. DE, *L'Ordre de Malte*. 2 vols, Vienne, 1889. (De Salles)

SCHERMERHORN, E., *Malta of the Knights*. London, 1929.
(Schermerhorn)

SCICLUNA, H. P., *The Church of St. John in Valletta*. Rome, 1955.
(Scicluna)

SPRETI, C., *Description of the Island of Malta*. Trans. with an Introduction and Notes by A. Mackenzie-Grieve. London, 1949.
(Spreti)

SUTHERLAND, A., *The Knights of Malta*. Edinburgh, 1830.
(Sutherland)

TAAFE, J., *History of the Order of St. John of Jerusalem*. London, 1852.
(Taafe)

TRIONFI, C., *Il Segno degli Eroi*. Milan, 1933.
(Trionfi)

VERTOT, L'ABBÉ DE, *Histoire des Chevaliers Hospitaliers de St. Jean de Jerusalem*. 2 vols, Paris, 1726.
(Vertot)

NOTES

PROLOGUE

1 and 2 ... Pius II, pp. 143–50.
    3 ... Atiya, pp. 131–32.
    4 ... Runciman, p. 123.
    5 ... Rossi II, p. 30.
    6 ... Fisher, p. 408.
7, 8 and 9 ... Fisher, pp. 404–05.
10 and 11 ... Runciman, p. xii.
    12 ... Ximenes, Archbishop of Toledo (1495–1517), Primate of Spain, Franciscan, reformer. The Church in Spain sorely needed reform. It had been found necessary to order that priests said Mass *once a year*. A kinsman of Ximenes was Grand Master of Malta (1773–75).
    13 ... Maximilian was styled 'Emperor-elect' in 1508 by Pope Julius II.

I. THE HOLY RELIGION

    1 ... D–B, p. 20.
    2 ... Luttrell in A.O.S.M., XX. 1.
    3 ... Finke III, pp. 198–99.
    4 ... Luttrell in A.O.S.M., XX. I
    5 ... Porter I, App. 6.
    6 ... Calnan in A.O.S.M., XXII. II.
    7 ... Porter I, pp. 288–89. The income of the English Grand Priory in 1338 was £3,826.4.6d, of which £2,280 was due to the Convent in Rhodes.
8 and 9 ... Hollister, p. 27.
    10 ... Calnan in A.O.S.M., XXII. II.
    11 ... De Salles, p. 338.
    12 ... Rossi I, pp. 13–20.

2. RHODES OF THE KNIGHTS

1 and 2 ... Med. Pilot, vol. IV, p. 335.

    3 ... The last native wild deer were slaughtered by the German garrison for food in World War II.

    4 ... Porter I, pp. 224–25.

    5 ... Bradford, p. 33.

    6 ... Porter I, pp. 337–38.

    7 ... Lionel Butler in A.O.S.M., XXIII. IV.

    8 ... Porter I, p. 346–47.

    9 ... Edmond Guiscard d'Estaing in A.O.S.M., XXII. IV.

3. MEN AND WEAPONS

1 and 2 ... C.N.M.H., p. 274, quoting L. Larchey, *The History of Bayard*.

3 and 4 ... D–B, pp. 50–51.

    5 ... Gautier, pp. 242–50.

    6 ... Luttrell in A.O.S.M., XX. I.

    7 ... Gautier, p. 12.

    8 ... Spreti, p. 4.

    9 ... C.N.M.H., p. 276, quoting W. Neade, *The Double Armed Man*.

    10 ... C.N.M.H., pp. 274–91.

    11 ... Gille, p. 221.

    12 ... Muller, pp. 197–216.

    13 ... Muller, App. p. 25, quoting M. Vallieres, *Dissertation on Countermines*.

    14 ... Grancsay, pp. 25–28.

    15 ... Runciman, p. 35.

    16 ... Porter, App. 8, p. 711, quoting Cotton MS.

    17 ... C.N.M.H., p. 282.

    18 ... Lib. Conc., Vol. 80, pp. 97, 104. Bosio II, p. 481. Galleys reduced to three 'sicut erat consuetudo' (1504).

4. THE SIEGE, 1480

1 ... A.O.S.M., XXII. I. This portrait is based on an even more fanciful picture in Bouhours (1676).

2 ... Pantaleone, pp. 127–40.

3 ... Bouhours, p. 2, gives the name of D'Aubusson's mother as 'Marguerite de *Comborn*'.

4 ... Porter I, p. 333 (my italics).

5 ... Runciman, p. 58.

6 ... Khidr: Muslim supernatural character approximating to Archangel Michael.

7 ... Porter I, p. 63.

8 ... Runciman, pp. 181–84.

9 ... Porter I, p. 342, quoting Caoursin.

10 ... Porter I, p. 342.

11 ... Dates vary wildly. Porter plays safe and quotes only two: 23rd May for the landing and 27th July for the attack on the Jews' Quarter. D'Aubusson gives 18th May for the opening of the siege and 25th July for the attack on the Jews' Quarter. Caoursin and De Curti agree on 23rd May for the landing. Pantaleone is a whole month out. Errors in conversion from the Latin calendar account for some of the differences.

12 ... De Curti says 'eight o'clock in the evening'.

13 ... Pauli, quoting Freher, *Rerum Germanicarum Scriptores*, vol. II, p. 158.

14 ... Lib. Bull., vol. IV, p. 16.

15 ... Many of the Ottoman professional miners came from the silver mines at Novo Brodo in Serbia (Runciman, p. 118).

16 ... His name appears as Gervaise Roger and as Roger Gervaise. Roger Jervis will suffice.

17 ... Porter says 200 gold ducats, or about £90. The ducat, zechino or sequin was about 9/-.

18 ... Only Pantaleone mentions this name which, as it happens, is an old and very common Maltese surname.

19 ... Gian Maria Filelfo, humanist and poet, who wrote an epic on the fall of Constantinople. He died in 1480.

20 ... Caoursin says 8,000 stakes, and that every Turk carried a length of cord with which to secure his prisoners.

D'Aubusson reports a similar story, but it seems more likely that the stakes were for abbatis and the cords for scaling work.

21 and 22 ... Details are based on Bosio, Vertot, Taafe, Porter, Sutherland and King, as well as Caoursin, De Curti and Pantaleone. They frequently disagree as to names which have been confused by latinization, translation and copying. For example, the German Johan von Aue appears as Giovanni D'Aw and John Dawe: the Englishman Anlaby appears as D'Avalos.

23 ... See Note 20 above.

24 ... Bosio II, pp. 339–40.

25 ... Mustafa Gelal-Zade. MS. in National Library, Vienna (Flügel II, no. 1067): 'Ta'rikh-i feth-i Radus', translated by Rossi (II, p. 29).

5. THE YEARS OF POWER, 1481–1521

1 ... Bosio II, p. 388.

2 ... The version of Djem's story is based on that of Caoursin and modified by reference to Burchard, Hammer and others, both pro- and anti-D'Aubusson.

3 ... Porter I, p. 392.

4 ... Porter I, p. 284.

5 ... Bosio II, p. 376.

6 ... Pauli II, p. 600, and Bottarelli I, pp. 255–56.

7 ... Parker, p. 60.

8 ... Parker, p. 61.

9 ... Parker, p. 96–97.

10 ... Parker, p. 120.

11 ... Pauli II, p. 411.

12 ... D'Aubusson reaped no personal benefit from his dealings with Djem. A Chapter General of 10th September 1489 at Rhodes voted the sum of 50,749 gold crowns to the Grand Master, to reimburse him for what he had spent in excess of the sum allowed for Djem's expenses. He had freely advanced this from the income allowed to him by his brother the Count of Monteil.

13 ... Lib. Bull., vol. 392, p. 174.

14 ... Bosio II, pp. 453–89.

15 ... Hughes, p. 67.

16 ... Bosio II, p. 489.

17 ... Lib. Conc., vol. 80, p. 59.

18 ... Bosio II, pp. 473–75.

19 ... Rossi I, p. 30.

20 ... Laiazzo was the ancient Aegae. There remain indications of its ancient importance – a fort, stone piers, a mole and the remains of a massive building which might have been a timber godown.

6. NOTHING SO WELL LOST, 1522

1 ... Schermerhorn, p. 29.

2 ... *See* pp. 107–8.

3 ... Atiya, p. 145.

4 ... Porter I, p. 420.

5 ... Letters of Suleiman and L'Isle Adam are from Pauli and Fontanus. Rossi II, p. 28, notes that Turkish sources make no mention of the correspondence; but Bosio II, pp. 529–30 and 541, reports it. Rossi thinks Fontanus' and Pauli's versions may be apocryphal; but confirms that Suleiman sent a 'Letter of Victory' or *Fethname* to Rhodes from Belgrade.

6 ... De Salles, I, App. 16, p. 364.

7 ... From the Italian translation of Rossi II, pp. 23–30.

8 ... Vertot VIII, p. 448.

9, 10, 11 ... Rossi II, pp. 29, 30.

12, 13, 14 ... Promis, pp. 42, 43, 49.

15 ... Bosio III, p. 21, and Promis, p. 51. In 1525 Tadini became a professed Knight and was awarded the rich Priory of Barletta, having assisted the Grand Master and his old friend Bosio in the negotiations which led to the Emperor's grant of Malta and Tripoli to the Holy Religion.

He next appears in action at Pavia, as general of the Emperor's artillery, in receipt of a 'stipend' of 2,000

NOTES

gold ducats per annum. In 1527, at Genoa, his elder
brother Girolamo was killed fighting at his side. In
1533 he retired on a pension of 666 gold ducats and
settled for three years at Martinengo. Worn out with a
lifetime of fighting and weakened by wounds, he sought
a dispensation, readily granted, to transfer his own and the
family property to his brother's son Camillo, and settled
in Venice, where he died 'of an apoplexy' in 1543 at the
relatively early age of sixty-three.

16 ... Bosio III, p. 57.
17 ... Trionfi, p. 193.
18 ... Bosio II, p. 159.
19 ... Rossi II, p. 48.
20 ... Details of the fighting are based on Bourbon, Bosio,
Vertot, Pantaleone, Fontanus and Sanudo, and Rossi's
translations, in Italian, of the Turkish of Mustafa Gelal-
Zade and Qara Celebi-Zade. The English versions of
Porter, Sutherland, Taafe and King have also been
referred to.
21 ... Rossi II, p. 16.
22 ... Trionfi describes Carpazio as a native of Trebizond.
'Basil the Karpathian', i.e. from Karpathos, or Scarpanto, is more likely.
23 ... Bosio II, p. 555, says the Turkish master gunner was
killed. Bourbon says he 'had his two legs shot off by a
ball from a culverin'. Turkish accounts agree that he
died.
24 ... Rossi II, p. 18.
25 ... Bosio II, pp. 557–64.
26 ... Bosio II, p. 564.
27 ... Rossi II, p. 19, and Bosio II, p. 569.
28 ... There is a good deal of confusion amongst narrators
about the assaults of 20th, 23rd and 24th September.
European sources rate Pir Mehmed's attack on the 20th
as the fiercest of the siege; but Turkish accounts are
clear that the general assault, for which Suleiman had a
ring-side seat specially erected, was on the 24th.
29 ... Porter's version (I, p. 465).
30 ... Rossi II, pp. 16, 19.

31 ... Vertot VIII, p. 448.

32 ... Bosio II, p. 573.

33 ... Vertot VIII, p. 451.

34 ... Vertot II, p. 423.

35 ... Lib. Bull., vol. 400, p. 224.

36 ... Fontanus, p. 269.

37 ... Porter I, p. 463. Bourbon, Vertot and Bosio agree that D'Amaral was tortured. Pantaleone says he was 'not tortured because of his high dignity and authority ... but he confessed that he had been moved by hatred because of the rebuff he had suffered by the election of Villiers de L'Isle Adam . . . he died *with many others* implicated by him during his trial'. Trionfi (pp. 284–90) follows Pantaleone (vol. VII, pp. 190–200).

38 ... The Italians, to whom Rhodes was assigned by the Treaty of Lausanne in 1923, made great efforts to restore the relics of the Knights – whom they regard as having a specially Italian significance. The Church of St. John was reconstructed some way distant from its original site. The Castello has been described as a 'monument to bad taste'.

The Franciscan monastery on Mount Phileremos, restored during the Italian régime, was again wrecked in 1945, during fighting between the Germans and Italians after Italy's capitulation to the Allies. In 1947 the sovereignty of Rhodes returned to Greece after six and a half centuries of foreign domination.

39 ... De Salles I, App. 16, p. 365.

40 ... From the Latin of Pantaleone (VII, p. 200).

41 ... Turkish sources insist that the first request for terms came from the Christians (Rossi II, p. 21) and that the 'Emir of Istankoi (Kos)' i.e. the Bailiff and Prior of St. Gilles, Prejan de Bidoux, was among the envoys.

42 ... This disagrees with Promis's statement that Tadini was sent away secretly.

43 ... Mustafa Gelal-Zade (Rossi II, p. 21) reports that a Christian deserter told Ahmed that the request for a truce was a stratagem to gain time. He also says that reinforcements actually arrived on 14th December. This

may be a reference to Fairfax's arrival, which, according to Bourbon, was on the 16th.

44 ... Porter I, p. 373.

45 ... Napoleon, after 'liberating' the richly bejewelled gold and silver frame, allowed the last Grand Master of Malta, Hompesch, to carry the Holy Ikon as well as the Hand of St. John with him into exile in 1798. After his forced abdication Hompesch sent the Hand and the Ikon to the Order's new Protector, Czar Paul. In 1917, again fabulously embellished, the relics were smuggled out of Russia and were last heard of in Belgrade in 1939.

46 ... Bosio II, pp. 588–89.

47 ... Rossi II, p. 42.

48 ... Bosio III, p. 8.

EPILOGUE

1 ... Rossi II, p. 42.

2 ... Rossi II, p. 51.

3 ... Rossi II, p. 39.

4 ... Rossi II, p. 51.

5 ... Runciman, p. 155.

6 ... Bosio III, p. 2.

7 ... The folklore of the Maltese has a number of interesting parallels with that of the Rhodians; but this may, of course, be due to earlier, common Hellenic (or Dorian) sources.

8 ... Bosio III, pp. 27, 105.

INDEX

Bourbon, Chevalier Jacques de, story of siege of Rhodes (1522), 2, 13, 48, 127, 130, 132–3, 136, 149, 152; and D'Amaral's trial, 142, 144, 145; and Turkish treatment of Christians, 154

Brusa, 8, 94

Bucciardo, Don Giorgio, Papal envoy, capture of, 101

Buck, Fra John, Turcopilier, 120; Commissioner for supplies, 121; death, 136, 138; use of gunpowder, 143

Budrum, 20, 35

Burchard, John, and Djem in Rome, 99, 100; and Djem's death, 102

Burgundy, 10, 12

Byzantine Empire, controlled by Islam, 7; schismatics, 8; defeated by Othman, 8; encircled by Turks, 10; and sovereignty of Order in Rhodes, 26

Candia, 119, 138, 148, 152; Tadini and, 123, 124

Caoursin, William, account of the siege of Rhodes (1480), 2, 63, 74, 75, 76, 79, 88–9, 90; ambassador to Papal court, 93; and treatment of Djem, 96, 102; apology for D'Aubusson, 103, 170 n. 12

Cape Kopria, 30

Cape Prasonisi, 30

Cape Voudhi, 31, 125

Capones, Ugo, 120

Caramania, 20, 94, 95

Cariati Bey, 104

Carpazio, Basil, penetrates Turkish lines, 128, 172 n. 22

Castellorizon, Egyptian attack on, 11, 27–8

Castile and Portugal, a Langue of the Order, 24, 104, 112; her Priories, 25; post of Pilier (Chancellor), 25; Langue allocation in Rhodes, 34; D'Amaral and, 104

Castrofilaco, Lucio, hanged for treason, 138–9, 140

Catalonia, war with Aragon, 11; absorbed by Spain, 12

Chaldiram, battle of, 110

Chambon, Lady Margaret, mother of D'Aubusson, 59, 169 n. 3

Charlemagne, his Hospital in Jerusalem, 15, 161

Charles V, Emperor, 117, 120; on fall of Rhodes, 155; sack of Rome, 158

Charles VIII, King of France, and Djem, 98, 100; invades Italy, 100; escapes homewards, 104

Chinese Empire, the Huing-Nu and, 8

Chios, 8, 105; Turkish occupation, 118, 122

Christendom, attitude to crusades in fifteenth century, 6; conflict with Islam, 7–8, 12; state of turmoil, 9, 12, 118; fails to help Rhodes, 12–14; feudal structure, 21; and Hospitallers' invincibility, 28

Christian Church, Greek, 13; position in Rhodes, 36; after Suleiman's victory, 157

Christian Church, Latin, and Papal schism, 9; and 'Henotikon', 10; used by conflicting powers, 12; and Greek Christians, 36; and English Protestants, 36; Muscovite hatred of, 117; conversion of churches to mosques, 157

Clement, Bishop of Rhodes, 119, 149

Clement V, Avignon Pope, 18; confirms Hospitallers' possession of Rhodes, 19

Clement VI, Avignon Pope, rebukes Hospitallers, 21

Clement VII, Pope, 2, 120, 158

Colyton, Sir Gervaise, at Tewkesbury, 23

Constantine XI, Emperor, death, 10; decree of 'Henotikon', 10, 36

Constantinople, fall of (1453), 1, 2, 10, 11–12, 22, 33, 37; siege of, 7, 44; sacked by Venice, 17; relations with Rhodes, 63, 64, 96, 104; proclaims Bajazet, 94; and spice trade, 108; Suleiman's entry, 157

Cornaro, Caterina, marriage to James III, 11

Cortoglu, corsair, 112–13, 115; Turkish chief of staff, 118, 121, 122; and siege of Rhodes (1522), 127, 130; bastinadoed, 131

Countermining, 46–8; use of in siege of Rhodes (1522), 128, 130, 131–4, 136–7, 143, 148

Crete, 8, 29, 53, 54; Tadini and, 123

Crusades, Pius II and, 6; fifteenth-century attitude to, 6; battle at Nicopolis, 9; capture of Acre, 17; fall of the Orders, 17; emulation by Charles VIII, 100; called by Alexander VI, 105

Cyprus, 29, 60; Egyptian tributary, 8, 11; Venetian protectorate, 11; Hospitallers in, 18–19, 161; allies of Rhodes, 27, 53

Damascus, 9, 27

D'Amaral, Andrea, 38, 104; and battle at Laiazzo, 107, 141; Grand Prior of Castile and Chancellor, 112, 121, 138; candidate for Grand Master, 112, 140, 141; and siege of Rhodes (1522), 120,

Di Saloma, Fra Paola, sent to Italy, 104
Di Scalenghe, Fra Ludovico, Admiral, 105
Djem, Ottoman pretender, 2, 58, 92, 154; claim to the throne, 94; seeks protection with the Order, 94; reception in Rhodes, 95–6; sent to France, 96, 98, 109; and the Order, 96–8; surrendered to Innocent VIII, 98–9, 103; reception in Rome, 99; Alexander VI and, 99–100; in custody with Charles VIII, 100–1; mystery of his death, 102, 104; responsibility for, 103–4
Docwra, Sir Thomas, 23; Captain General of the Galleys, 105; Grand Prior of England, 112; candidate for Grand Master, 112
Dodecanese, the, 18, 29
Ducaut-Bourget, F., Rule of the Order in Rhodes, 39–40
Dupuis, Marie, and vulnerability of Rhodes, 34–5
Du Puy, Raymond, Master of the Hospital, 16; his original Rule, 16

Egypt, 7, 8, 20; counter-crusade, 10–11; commercial interests, 11; attacks on Rhodes, 11, 28, 106; treaty between Order and Mamelukes, 27, 93; attacks Castellorizon, 27–8; harassment of her shipping, 93; war with Ottomans, 104; loss of the Mogarbina, 106–7; and battle at Laiazzo, 107–8; defeated and annexed by Selim, 109–10, 113; Turkish governors, 121, 145
El Hakim, Caliph, sack of Jerusalem, 15
England, 118; struggle with France, 9; failure to assist Rhodes, 13; feudal responsibility of Knights, 21, 22; income of Grand Priory, 22, 167 n. 7; position of Grand Prior, 22; a Langue of the Order, 22, 24; her Priories, 25; post of Pilier (Turcopilier); Langue allocation in Rhodes, 34, 74, 129, 133, 134, 136, 137, 148, 149; mercenaries from, 42; casualties at sieges, 89, 138; relief force from, 136–7; title of the Order of St. John, 161
Ephesus, defeat of Ottoman fleet, 27
Erasmus, Desiderius, on Julius II, 106
Escarrieros, Tomas, commander of Spanish bastion, 120
Europe, 1; eastern unity under Jagiellos, 13; religious reformers, 13; passage to Rhodes, 53, 54, 71, 72; shift in balance of power, 104
Euthemios, Metropolitan, 158

Fairfax, Fra Nicholas, 138, 148, 152
Feracle, 19, 35
Ferdinand of Aragon, marriage to Isabella of Castile, 12; and Charles VIII, 100
Ferhad Pasha, and Shah-Suwar, 121, 122
Filelfo, Gian Maria, secretary to D'Aubusson, 80, 169 n. 19
Fisher, H. A. L., History of Europe, 8, 9, 10
Florence, collapse of her banks, 21; welcomes Charles VIII, 100; engineers from, 129
Fontanus, Jacobus, story of siege of Rhodes (1522), 2, 133; judge of Apellate Court, 141; and D'Amaral, 144
Fornari, Domenico, Genoese captain, 119
Fornovo, battle of, 104
France, struggle with England, 9; domination of western Europe, 12; acquisitions, 12; failure to assist Rhodes, 13; feudal responsibilities of Knights, 21; a Langue of the Order, 24; her Priories, 24; post of Pilier (Hospitaller), 25; and election of Grand Master, 26; Langue allocation in Rhodes, 34, 67, 78, 100, 104; gunnery experts, 42; Djem at Bourgeneuf, 96, 98; and spice trade, 108; conflict with Spain, 117
Francis I, King of France, 115, 120
Franciscans, 90, 106; in Rhodes, 74–5, 93, 135; monastery on Mount Phileremos, 173 n. 38
Franks, 7, 10, 18
Frapan, George (Master George), traitor, 56, 63; and the campaign, 66, 67; deserts Turkish army, 70, 75, 80, 81–2; death, 82
Frederick III, Emperor, 2, 67

Gautier, L., Chivalry, 40
Gelal-Zade, Mustafa, account of siege of Rhodes (1522), 3, 92, 145, 154, 170 n. 25, 173 n. 43; justifies Suleiman, 116
Genoa, Mediterranean possessions, 8; and Turkish menace, 10; Egyptian war with, 11; use of gunpowder mine, 46; and siege of Rhodes (1522), 119, 130
Gentile, Andreotto, commander of Italian bastion, 120
Gerard, Blessed, founds an Augustinian Order, 15–16; and title of Hospitallers of St. John, 16
Germany, principalities, 13, 117; rise of nationalism, 13; a Langue of the Order, 24; her Priories, 25; post of Pilier (Grand Bailiff), 25; Langue allocation in Rhodes, 34, 129; gunnery experts, 42, 129